W9-BGN-706

A Mile in Her Shoes
Lessons From the Lives
of Old Testament Women

Sisters
Bible Study for Women

A Mile in Her Shoes

Lessons From the Lives of Old Testament Women

Participant's Workbook

Sheron C. Patterson

Abingdon Press / Nashville

SISTERS

A MILE IN HER SHOES: LESSONS FROM THE LIVES OF OLD TESTAMENT WOMEN

Copyright © 2005 by Abingdon Press

All rights reserved.

No part of this work may be reproduced or transmitted in any form or by any means, electronic or mechanical, including photocopying and recording, or by means of any information storage or retrieval system, except as may be expressly permitted by the 1976 Copyright Act or in writing from the publisher. Requests for permission should be addressed in writing to Abingdon Press, 201 Eighth Avenue South, Nashville, TN 37203, or e-mail: permissions@abingdonpress.com.

This book is printed on recycled, acid-free, elemental-chlorine free paper.

Library of Congress Cataloging-in-Publication Data

Library of Congress Cataloging-in-Publication Data

Patterson, Sheron C., 1959-
  A mile in her shoes : lessons from the lives of Old Testament women : participant's workbook / Sheron C. Patterson.
    p. cm.
  ISBN 0-687-74111-4 (alk. paper)
  1. Women in the Bible--Biography. 2. Bible. O.T.--Biography. 3. African American women--Religious life. I. Title.

  BS575.P28 2005
  221.9'22--dc22
                              2005000157

Scripture quotations, unless otherwise indicated, are from the New Revised Standard Version of the Bible, copyright 1989, by the Division of Christian Education of the National Council of the Churches of Christ in the United States of America. Used by permission. All rights reserved.

Scripture quotations marked (RSV) are from the *Revised Standard Version of the Bible,* copyright 1946, 1952, 1971 by the Division of Christian Education of the National Council of the Churches of Christ in the United States of America. Used by permission. All rights reserved.

Scripture quotations marked (NIV) are taken from the HOLY BIBLE, NEW INTERNATIONAL VERSION ®. Copyright 1973, 1978, 1984 by International Bible Society. Used by permission of Zondervan Publishing House. All rights reserved.

06 07 08 09 10 11 12 13 14 — 10 9 8 7 6 5 4 3 2

MANUFACTURED IN THE UNITED STATES OF AMERICA

For my mother,

Johnsie Jackson Covington

Contents

WEEK SIX: THE WIDOW WITH THE OIL—HANGING ON UNTIL YOUR MIRACLE COMES

Introduction

From the moment Eve stepped onto the earth, women have been a fascinating part of the biblical landscape. Women of all types fill the pages of the Bible and add a dimension of the feminine to the Word of God. In the Bible there are women who are both named and unnamed. There are rich women and poor women, married women and women without husbands. Some women are limited to the periphery of the action, leaving us the task of piecing together their identities, while the complete stories of others are recounted in rich detail. Regardless of the length of their stories, all of the women in this study are contributors to the testimony of the goodness and awesome power of God.

However, we should never make the mistake of dismissing biblical women as ancient, outdated relics. They are our foremothers. We are the daughters of Ruth, Esther, and Mary. We are linked to them through the blood of Jesus Christ. They deserve our homage, respect, and love for being who they were and for living when they did. We, as Christian women, would not be who we are today, if they had not lived such powerful lives of faith thousands of years ago. Their courageous acts of believing in God, in spite of the consequences, make them perennial "she-roes."

A MILE IN HER SHOES focuses on women of the Old Testament who resided in ancient Palestine, a hot and arid land of mountains, deserts, and valleys. Here we find a remarkable cadre of women who lived during the time of prophets, kings, and judges. These were smart, brave, shrewd, and wise women. If they had wealthy husbands or fathers, they wore silk and linen robes complete with golden earrings and bracelets. If they were from poor families, their garments were made of a coarser fabric and their jewelry was silver and bronze.

These women lived under patriarchal rule where men made all of the decisions. Women had no authority and were considered the property of their father, husband, or brother. Girls were not educated in schools or classes but were expected to marry and raise families. Old Testament women led busy lives that were limited to their homes since they performed most of the work there. They ground the grain to make flour; hauled water from the town well; harvested crops; kept a fire burning in the hearth; spun thread to weave fabric; used the fabric to make the family's clothing; and nursed, washed, and cared for their children.

The six Old Testament women in A MILE IN HER SHOES were chosen because I find their lives especially compelling and instructive. I have chosen not to highlight only high-profile women whose stories are well known, so some of the stories included here may be new to you. I did not select women with predictable narratives and fairy-tale lives. Rather, each has an authentic testimony, complete with trials and tribulations. From start to finish, each woman is a role model for holding onto our faith. Their tenacity is admirable. Their lives are our classrooms. My hope is that you will experience the emotion and the drama that accompanied their faith journeys. I want you to cry with them when they ache and laugh with them when they rejoice.

Let's walk a mile in the shoes of these six memorable women. First is *Deborah,* a woman who worked outside her home as a judge, a rare occurrence in the biblical drama. She became a warrior for the Lord. Next is *Rahab* the prostitute. Don't be shocked. Her story shows us that God can transform us, raising us from any depth to heights we never imagined. *Hagar,* in Week Three, was the Bible's first single parent. Her saga of travail and triumph demonstrates what God can do. The following week, we look at *Abigail,* who found herself unequally yoked in her marriage. Her faith in God was put to the test, but she ultimately triumphed with God's help. *Hannah* was barren and prayed to God for a child. Her relentless quest emboldens us. We conclude with *the widow with the oil,* who appeared to be out of luck and headed for disaster. Yet, her faithful obedience saved her family.

The goal of A MILE IN HER SHOES is to help you experience the intense level of belief and commitment that these six Old Testament women possessed. The readings for each day immerse us in the story of their lives. Day One of each week offers an overview of each woman and her special circumstances. Moreover, there is a listing of the entire Scripture passage to be read during the week. I suggest that you read the full passage on Day One in order to grasp the featured woman's complete story. On Day Two through Day Six, the readings and Scripture text highlight specific segments of each woman's life for your consideration. In addition, Day Six offers an opportunity to put yourself—as much as possible—in each woman's shoes, imagining what it was like to be her and learning from her strength and faithfulness.

On Day Seven you will meet with your group. In preparation for the meeting, you are encouraged to think about what you might like to share with your group members. Questions for reflection are suggested.

Each day's reading is also followed by questions for reflection. I hope these questions will encourage you to engage what you have learned about these women with your own spiritual journey. So please get a pencil or pen and write your thoughts in the workbook. There are no right or wrong answers, just your thoughts and your comments about these profound women of faith. Finally, I recommend beginning and ending each day's time of study with prayer. Beginning and ending with God will help us follow the strong examples set by the women in the study.

Having been a pastor for two decades, I am very familiar with the journey to become all that God calls us to be. I am on the same journey myself! I have an enthusiastic interest in women of faith and their experiences, which has manifested itself into several books, radio and television broadcasts, support groups, and a thriving counseling practice. Throughout the book I share portions of my own experiences with some of the women I have encountered as a means of letting you know that we are all in this together.

A well-known saying is that you never know what someone is like until you walk a mile in her shoes. Now is your opportunity to walk with and be blessed by these six servants of God.

Week One: Deborah—Lessons on Leadership

Readings for the Week: Judges 4:1-23; 5:1-3

DAY ONE: RISING UP IN OPPRESSIVE TIMES

Judges 4:1-3

The Israelites again did what was evil in the sight of the LORD, after Ehud died. So the LORD sold them into the hand of King Jabin of Canaan, who reigned in Hazor; the commander of his army was Sisera, who lived in Harosheth-ha-goiim. Then the Israelites cried out to the LORD for help; for he had nine hundred chariots of iron, and had oppressed the Israelites cruelly twenty years.

God moves in mysterious ways. Hardships and hard times can be God's catalyst for positive change. Leaders are produced in difficult times. Who would think that the reign of an oppressive king like Jabin would generate a leader like Deborah? Jabin was the Canaanite king, and Sisera was his cruel army commander. Sisera was infamous for the violence that his nine hundred iron chariots produced. The Israelites were allowed to suffer greatly at the hands of Sisera because they were being punished by God. The first few verses of Chapter 4 tell their story: "The Israelites again did what was evil in the sight of the LORD. . . . So the LORD sold them into the hand of King Jabin of Canaan" (verses 1-2). Despite this punishment, God was also merciful. God elevated the capable Deborah to lead during these hard times, and her leadership significantly influenced the people to return to God.

In the midst of the oppression, God appointed Deborah to be a leader by serving as a judge. She was one of six judges who guided Israel after the time of the patriarchs and before the time of kings. She was probably the only female judge because women in her society were not permitted to have leadership roles. Old Testament judges were different from the judges we see in our legal system today. They were not elected or officially appointed. They were selected by God from the general population to rule the people and lead them back to righteousness. They served as administrators who helped organize and facilitate the workings of the community. They settled disputes and administered justice. In times of threat, they helped mobilize the Israelite armies to fight. Therefore their tasks were both political and religious; and their leadership helped insure the social, religious, and political stability.

Deborah demonstrates how we can take the negative situations in our lives and use them to propel rather than sink us. It has been said that birds, such as eagles, effectively gain their altitude when they ascend against resistant winds. Aerodynamically the colliding forces lift the birds higher into the skies. Birds do not fear resistance; instead they use it to their advantage. So can we.

Attributes such as power, presence, and persistence may be common during good times, but what about when lives are at stake? We are human; and during difficult times our survival instinct says, *Go hide and ride out the storms until safety comes.* Safety makes us relax, while trouble makes us tense.

Deborah shows us how to lead despite challenging conditions. God has the proven ability to turn the unfavorable into the favorable. You too are a leader. Leaders come in all shapes and sizes, and are assigned tasks both large and small. You have the God-given ability to lead others, or maybe yourself, out of a bad situation. However you must seize this power with faith, just as Deborah did.

Reflecting and Recording

Do you agree that turbulent times create leaders? If so, make a list of characteristics that hard times produce in leaders.

Are you facing a difficult situation in your own life that may prompt you into leadership? What will be required of you to step forward?

Have you ever hidden or run from trouble? Why? Looking back, how could you have changed the situation?

DAY TWO: EFFECTIVE LEADERS ARE IN TOUCH WITH GOD

Judges 4:4-7

*At that time Deborah, a prophetess, wife of Lappidoth was judging Israel.
She used to sit under the palm of Deborah between Ramah and Bethel
in the hill country of Ephraim; and the Israelites came up to her for judgment.
She sent and summoned Barak son of Abinoam from Kedesh in Naphtali,
and said to him, "The LORD, the God of Israel, commands you, 'Go, take
position at Mount Tabor, bringing ten thouand from the tribe of Naphtali
and the tribe of Zebulun. I will draw out Sisera, the general of Jabin's
army, to meet you by the Wadi Kishon with his chariots and his troops;
and I will give him into your hand.' "*

Are you busy? Do you have a checklist of places to go, things to do, and people to see all day, every day? You are not alone. I confess that sometimes I wonder if I am coming or going. Full, vigorous lives characterize many women's daily routine. Despite our modern conveniences, we still strain to accomplish all of our daily assignments. Even though our lives are full, there is still room to be a leader, especially one in touch with God.

We can ascertain from the day's text that Deborah was in touch with God despite probably having a busy daily agenda. We know that she was a prophetess, a wife, a mother, and a judge, who kept regular office hours under "the palm of Deborah between Ramah and Bethel" (verse 5). As a judge she made decisions and settled disputes for her people. Imagine the line outside her office. First perhaps was the camel herder who felt the merchant was mistreating him. Next maybe were two landowners who had a border dispute. They all came to Deborah with their problems because she was a person with godly answers.

In the midst of this work, Deborah heard from God that she was to summon the warrior, Barak, into battle against the Canaanites. She heard this godly command because she was connected to God, and she valued what God had to say. We too must be connected to God if we are to hear God's instructions for us. Not only did Deborah hear, but she responded with obedience. Being in touch with God makes all the difference.

Are you connected to God? Imagine if we each had a mechanism that monitored the level of our contact with God. It would be a built-in device that scanned our godly connection. It would hum peacefully when all was well, or blare loudly when we were not as close as we should be. Since we don't have such a device, we must monitor ourselves. I'm not suggesting a sterile piece of equipment but rather an ongoing check that monitors our faith connection. We must continually ask: Have I prayed today? Have I read the Bible today? Have I had a conversation with God today? If we have not been in touch with God, there will be indications such as grumpiness, unexplained anger, and hopelessness. If we have been in touch with God, the bumps and bruises of the day will not hurt us as much as they might absent God's nearness.

Whether our task is to lead groups of people out of a crisis or organize our church's next potluck, we need to be in touch with God. Deborah's godly connection enabled her to play a major role in God's kingdom. When we put God first, all of our other concerns will be met. Begin to check in with God often during the day. If necessary, schedule time with God on your daily planner or calendar. Seek a never-ending conversation with God as you flow through your responsibilities.

Reflecting and Recording

If you monitored your connection with God, what would be the results? What are some of the outward signs of your internal connection?

Why does being busy hinder our relationship with God? What things do you need to remove from your life in order to spend more time with God?

Have you ever attempted to be a leader without God's power in your life? What was the result?

DAY THREE: FLEXIBLE LEADERS UNDERSTAND CHANGE

Judges 4:8-9

Barak said to her, "If you will go with me, I will go; but if you will not go with me, I will not go." And she said, "I will surely go with you; nevertheless, the road on which you are going will not lead to your glory, for the LORD will sell Sisera into the hand of a woman." Then Deborah got up and went with Barak to Kedesh.

Barak insisted that Deborah accompany him into battle, even though the initial request was for him to go alone. Deborah was able to handle the change of plan because she was flexible. Leaders understand that a change of plans can occur when you least expect it. Deborah may have been startled by the request, but she was flexible and able to adapt. Change can catch us off guard sometimes, and change has the ability to knock us off balance. Our relationship with God gives us the needed stability.

I once had a poster prominently displayed on my office wall that read: "Blessed are the flexible, for they shall not be bent out of shape." These are priceless words of wisdom for anyone but particularly for women who serve as leaders. The original plans may change. The original people may not be around when the plan is executed. In such situations change is inevitable. We cannot allow ourselves to be paralyzed by change, but need to find ways to be energized by it.

Change is not something that people like. In fact, prevailing opinion says that "no one likes change but a baby with a wet diaper." The old ways seem much more comfortable and familiar. Change threatens what we know and believe to be true. I've seen churches turned into battlefields over change. I know you have too.

Even minor changes can throw us into a tizzy if we let them. Let me offer a confession about change. When my neighborhood grocery store changed its checkout system, I was thrown for a loop. When I had shopped the previous week, the cashier took my groceries from my basket, scanned them, and bagged them. The following week, the cashier's job description and equipment had been changed. Suddenly, I had to lift my groceries from the basket and place them on a conveyor belt that reached the clerk. It was a minor change, but it bothered me. I wanted the grocery store to stay the same and was flustered by the change. When something is new and different it causes us to react.

There will always be changes—in your family, work, or church. Something that helps me handle change is the belief that God is with me every step of the way, that I am not alone. God is faithful, and God's promises are true. The beautiful hymn, "Great Is Thy Faithfulness," reminds us that there is a constant source of goodness in God, that God never changes or fails us.

I am comforted by the realization of God's unchanging goodness and constant presence. Moreover, I believe that resisting change can inadvertently be a means of resisting God. Resisting can create fear and confusion. When we fight for the old way and rail against the new, we may in fact be hindering a new movement of God. If we trust in God, what is there to fear?

Where would the Israelites be if Deborah had fought and resisted change? I believe that she embraced and accepted change because she was sure that God was in it. The lesson here is that we must have the faith to embrace change, even invite change. We must leave behind our rigid and stiff mindset and become pliable for God's service.

Reflecting and Recording

What types of changes bother you the most? List them and prayerfully consider whether or not you are hindering or helping the movement of God in your life.

Think about a time when your lack of flexibility prevented you from being the leader God planned. What could you have done differently? What did you learn from that situation that will make you more open and adaptable to new challenges and opportunities?

How can God help you with your flexibility toward change?

DAY FOUR: SUCCESSFUL LEADERS WORK COOPERATIVELY WITH MALE CO-WORKERS

Judges 4:10

Barak summoned Zebulun and Naphtali to Kedesh; and ten thousand warriors went up behind him; and Deborah went up with him.

Deborah agreed to Barak's request and accompanied him on the God-inspired journey. She worked cooperatively with him, and they became a team. When life places us in circumstances requiring teamwork, it is vital to rely on God. Our feelings can be fickle and erratic. God, however, is a steady, reliable source who, we can be assured, will complete the task.

The notion of teaming with a man for battle may have been a stretch for Deborah. Women were rarely seen on the battlefields of the Old or New Testament. Even rarer were male/female partnerships beyond marriage. But Deborah agreed to this unlikely alliance because the cause of liberating her people no doubt outweighed any personal objections and fears. This noble cause also overrode the cultural practices that kept men and women separate. She had to keep her focus on God. This may have helped her handle any sexism that she encountered from the men in her community.

Unfortunately, even today there are some who discriminate against and devalue women. These people are misled. The key to gender cooperation is knowing and understanding our variations. Men and women are not socialized the same way, in most instances. These differences are not bad, just distinctive; and in their own way they make life exciting. *Men Are from Mars, Women Are from Venus,* by John Gray, speaks in simple terms about the complex differences between men and women. Reading this book helped me develop a greater appreciation of both genders.

God does not intend for us to be intimidated or threatened by men or vice versa—that would destroy God's plan of unity. Deborah may not have been able to articulate this, but I would suggest that in order for women to work successfully with men, they must have a strong relationship with God. We must see ourselves as God sees us, equal to men, yet not better than them. We must build and maintain a strong sense of self and be confident in ourselves as women. Confidence in our abilities enables us to take on leadership roles.

As a pastor, I work most often with male colleagues. This is rarely an issue for me because I am so accustomed to it. In conversations with laity, people occasionally ask, What is it like to be the only woman? I use such instances to share my perspective on men. I consider men as my co-creations, made by God. In Genesis we are told that God created male and female in God's image (Genesis 1:26). This means both genders reflect God's image, even though men and women are vastly different. When men and women partner as teammates on projects, our ability to collaborate celebrates God's design.

Reflecting and Recording

What are some of the differences between men and women? How does God make those differences complimentary?

Why are some men and women intimidated by the opposite gender?

What are some of the issues that arise from the differences between women and men in the workplace? Have you experienced difficulties working on projects with men? What did you learn from this situation?

DAY FIVE: LEADERS KNOW HOW TO ENCOURAGE

Judges 4:14-23

Then Deborah said to Barak, "Up! For this is the day on which the LORD has given Sisera into your hand. The LORD is indeed going out before you." So Barak went down from Mount Tabor with ten thousand warriors following him. And the LORD threw Sisera and all his chariots and all his army into a panic before Barak; Sisera got down from his chariot and fled away on foot, while Barak pursued the chariots and the army to Harosheth-ha-goiim. All the army of Sisera fell by the sword; no one was left.
Now Sisera had fled away on foot to the tent of Jael wife of Heber the Kenite; for there was peace between King Jabin of Hazor and the clan of Heber the Kenite. Jael came out to meet Sisera, and said to him, "Turn aside, my lord, turn aside to me; have no fear." So he turned aside to her into the tent, and she covered him with a rug. Then he said to her, "Please give me a little water to drink; for I am thirsty." So she opened a skin of milk and gave him a drink and covered him. He said to her, "Stand at the entrance of the tent, and if anybody comes and asks you, 'Is anyone here?' say, 'No.'" But Jael wife of Heber took a tent peg, and took a hammer in her hand, and went softly to him and drove the peg into his temple, until it went down into the ground—he was lying fast asleep from weariness—and he died. Then, as Barak came in pursuit

of Sisera, Jael went out to meet him, and said to him, "Come, and I will show you the man whom you are seeking." So he went into her tent; and there was Sisera lying dead, with the tent peg in his temple. So on that day God subdued King Jabin of Canaan before the Isralites. Then the hand of the Israelites bore harder and harder on King Jabin of Canaan, until they destroyed King Jabin of Canaan.

Deborah loudly encouraged Barak with the word *Up!* What power and belief in God she possessed! Sitting together in the pre-battle preparation, she may have glanced at him and realized he was feeling discouraged. Maybe the soldiers that they assembled did not seem brave and valiant. If she had articulated irritation and anger with words such as, "What's wrong with you?" or "I know you are not getting scared now," the mission may have been a disaster. Rather, she demonstrated the traits of an encourager, which include unselfishness and being undeterred by any negative responses. Deborah shows us that encouragers have their eyes on God, and they speak with an almost future-tense faith.

Encouragers look beyond the current situation. The situation may have been tense and frightening as they began their journey. Deborah offered encouragement to Barak, and together they were victorious. She was not resting in her own power, but using all that came from God.

It is amazing how an uplifting word can shake us loose when *down* won't let us go. Jesus had encouraging words for those who were afflicted and downtrodden. He searched for those who felt left out and offered them hope. The Beatitudes are Jesus' blessings or encouragers for the hurting. He says in Luke 6:20-23:

> Blessed are you who are poor, / for yours is the kingdom of God. / Blessed are you who are hungry now, / for you will be filled. / Blessed are you who weep now, / for you will laugh. / Blessed are you when people hate you, and when they exclude you, revile you, and defame you on account of the Son of Man! Rejoice in that day and leap for joy, for surely your reward is great in heaven. . . .

Can you speak a fresh word of encouragement, hope, and energy to someone who needs to hear it? When others listen to you, are they encouraged or discouraged? Think about that for a moment. There is amazing power in the gift of encouragement, a gift we all possess. We should not rely on pastors and other speakers to always be the encouragers. You are an encourager too. Moreover, encouragement is a form of leadership. God has designed your circle of influence to include people whom only you can reach. I may not be able to influence them, but you can. Your words, your tone of voice, or your perspective may be able to penetrate their hearing like no one else can.

For example, when I was in training for my first 5K run, I secured the services of a running coach. He was a marathon runner with a knack for helping rookies like me. There were numerous assistance options available to me, ranging from books to videos on running; but I knew that I respond best to a voice that pushes me positively. During the race, he barked out just the right words and phrases that connected with my ability to run. His encouragement prompted me to be my best. I did not win the race, but, hallelujah, I completed the race.

Make it a priority to learn how to encourage others. This world of ours is thirsty for a word of hope about what we can do in Jesus' name. The apostle Paul wrote, "I can do all things through him who strengthens me" (Philippians 4:13).

Reflecting and Recording

How can you help someone believe that they can be successful in the name of Jesus? List the people or situations needing your encouragement. How will you try to offer encouragement?

What kinds of encouragement are effective for you?

Why did Jesus choose to write about hurting people in the Beatitudes? How does that reference influence your understanding of hurting people?

DAY SIX: LEADERS ARE GRATEFUL FOR THEIR VICTORIES

Judges 5:1-3

Then Deborah and Barak son of Abinoam sang on that day, saying:
"When locks are long in Israel,
when the people offer themselves willingly—
bless the LORD!
"Hear, O kings; give ear, O princes;
to the LORD I will sing,
I will make melody to the LORD, the God of Israel."

I imagine Deborah and Barak returning home with wide smiles after battle. Their shoulders are thrown back, their heads are high, and all is well. They are weary and worn, but ecstatic about the victory. The battle was won, the enemy vanquished. Specifically, Sisera, the commander of the army, was dead; and Jabin, the Canaanite king, had been destroyed. The hard work was behind them. But notice what they did next: They sang praises to God.

Their song celebrated what God had done. They were grateful for bold leaders and receptive followers. Both are necessary for success—on the battlefield, a work project, or church program. Most important, both came from God's goodness.

We may not be able to celebrate our victories at all. There may be the inability to recognize the good things in our midst. Can you accept compliments? Sometimes we as women shun compliments because we feel it puts too much attention on us. Sometimes shame gets in the way. The problems of the past won't allow us to revel in the successes of today. I encountered a woman once who was not able to celebrate her victories and accomplishments. Even though she worked diligently on programs and ministries, she refused to applaud or celebrate her own success. The ability to savor victories is vital.

Only a heart filled with gratitude can sing about God's goodness. Gratitude is a requirement for us as leaders because it reflects the way we feel about God. Thankfulness is expected from God. It says that we recognize who God is. Gratitude is also about joy. Grateful people are joyful people. They are able to look back and see all that God has done for them. This enables them to look ahead with hope and anticipation.

When we keep God at the center of our praise, we are mindful of who is really the source of our blessings. Never would we want to usurp God's power and accomplishments. What we want to avoid is being ego-centered. One definition of *ego* is "Edging God Out." It is possible to push God out when we experience victory. We may accidentally push God out on numerous occasions by lauding ourselves rather than God, who is the true source of our gifts and successes.

Deborah came home singing. She was not ashamed of herself or her God. What about you?

Reflecting and Recording

Why do some people struggle with patting themselves on the back? Does that deny God's grace, and if so, how?

Have you ever been guilty of edging God out (EGO)? If so, how did you correct it?

Spend time today reflecting on what it was like to be Deborah. Write a few sentences that describe her acts of leadership and how you too can be a leader.

DAY SEVEN: GROUP MEETING

Prepare for the meeting by thinking back over your readings and reflections for the week and what you would like to share with the group. You might ponder such questions as these:

♦ As you imagined what it would be like to walk a mile in this woman's shoes, what lessons have you learned from studying the story of this remarkable biblical woman?

♦ How were you strengthened as well as challenged by this story?

♦ What insights have you gained about God from reading about this woman and her relationship with God? How did God act in her life? How has God acted in similar ways in your own life?

♦ What have these stories inspired you to do? How will you put what you have learned into practice?

Pray for the members of your group. Pray that you will be open and receptive to hearing what they have to say as well as what God is saying to you in your time together.

Week Two:
Rahab—Moving
From the Gutter to Glory

Readings for the Week: Joshua 2:1-24; 6:17, 22-25

DAY ONE: A PART OF GOD'S PLAN

Joshua 2:1

Then Joshua son of Nun sent two men secretly from Shittim as spies, saying, "Go, view the land, especially Jericho."

Walking a mile in the shoes of Rahab is perhaps the most perilous journey of all the women in this study. She was chosen because she tests us. Let's be honest, sometimes we women of faith can become haughty and pious. We devalue others who don't look like us, live like us, or act like us. Yet our faith informs us that God is at work at all times—even in the life of a prostitute!

The life of an Old Testament prostitute must have been harrowing by any standard. Prostitution is the same today as it was then: the exchange of sex for money or goods. Some Bible versions give Rahab the title of harlot. Either title—harlot or prostitute—describes a woman whose behavior was despised by the religious community and decried in the Bible. For example, we find a warning in Proverbs 5:1-4 to avoid such women: "My son be attentive to my wisdom. . . . / For the lips of a loose woman drip honey, / and her speech is smoother than oil; / but in the end she is bitter as wormwood."

The fact that God selected and used Rahab for good is a vital point. Many would consider her unusable for the Kingdom. Not much is known about her personally in the early stages of her life. We know that she was a Canaanite (people who worshiped idols). We also know that she had three strikes against her: (1) she was a woman; (2) she was an outsider; and (3) she was a prostitute. Rahab's life illustrates that God moves even in bleak, unsavory situations; and God uses and blesses whomever God deems appropriate. Even the most blatant sinner is not outside of God's reach.

Rahab was remarkably ready to become a part of God's plan. In this text God positioned Rahab to be in the right place at the right time, intersecting God's divine will for her life and the lives of others. Joshua, the new leader of the Israelite people, is energized as he leads the people to dispossess the Canaanites from their land. As the Israelites moved into the new land, they were commanded to kill all of the foreigners. In today's text Joshua sends out his men to spy on the walled city of Jericho before they seize it. Once the spies enter Jericho, they unexplainably go directly to Rahab's house and spend the night. We have no concrete reports of what happened during the visit, just innuendo. Some versions of the Bible indicate that the men "lay" with her, suggesting that a business transaction occurred. Regardless of the fleshly concerns, God turned a place of ill repute into a safe haven for the Israelite spies.

When we describe Rahab as marginalized because of her occupation, we mean that she was pushed to the edge of society and made to feel unimportant. This was illustrated by where she lived—on the outskirts of the city, far away from respectable people. Rahab's home was actually built into the walls of Jericho. Her home was on public view for all to see. Those who came and went did so under the scrutiny of others. That's how people knew that the two spies were there. News traveled fast in her day—even without the Internet! Soon there was a knock at the door from the king's messengers. The king demanded that Rahab turn over the spies. He knew that they had come to "search out all the land." Instead of handing them over, Rahab hid them on her roof and told the king's men that the spies had escaped through the city's gates before they were closed at dark.

Rahab was a part of God's plan in an unlikely way. She teaches us that we never know when, how, or where God may penetrate our surroundings and turn them into a blessing. She shows us that we can never do anything so bad that we are outside of the grasp of God's forgiveness. The location of her home was the outskirts. The people of Jericho disregarded her. However, God placed her on center stage. Isn't that just like God?

What about you? If you have ever felt unworthy of God's love because of a past sin, Rahab's story offers witness that God's power and forgiveness overshadow any negatives we may have in our pasts.

Reflecting and Recording

Have you ever felt outside of God's protective love? How did you feel? When and how did God show you otherwise?

Why do you think the scouts went directly to Rahab's house?

Why do Christians sometimes look down on those who live morally corrupt lives? What should our response be?

DAY TWO: TRANSFORMING BEFORE OUR EYES

Joshua 2:9-11

*"I know that the L*ORD* has given you the land, and that dread of you
has fallen on us, and that all the inhabitants of the land melt in fear
before you. For we have heard how the L*ORD* dried up the water
of the Red Sea before you when you came out of Egypt, and what you did
to the two kings of the Amorites that were beyond the Jordan,
to Sihon and Og, whom you utterly destroyed. As soon as we heard it,
our hearts melted, and there was no courage left in any of us because of you.
The L*ORD* your God is indeed God in heaven above and on earth below."*

Before our very eyes, Rahab is transformed from the harlot of the city
to a believer in Yahweh, who recited the great deeds of the Lord! Look
at the timing of her statements. They come after she has successfully rescued the Israelite spies. On the roof of her house, with no prompting,
she begins what appears to be a heartfelt soliloquy. She reveals that the
entire city is afraid of the oncoming Israelites. Specifically, two divine
acts—the drying up of the Red Sea and the slaughter of two Amorite
kings—have her and the other Jericho residents melting in fear. Most
important, she goes on to acknowledge that the Israelite God is supreme
by declaring that Yahweh is truly, "God in heaven above and on the
earth below."

Rahab's transformation included (1) acknowledging God and (2) sparing the lives of the two spies. Both carried heavy penalties in her society. First, she was a pagan Canaanite; Yahweh was not one of the gods her people worshiped. Second, she was a resident of Jericho. The king would have instantly killed her and the spies had they been discovered. She had committed treason by harboring them.

Interestingly Rahab had two different sets of men with opposing purposes under her roof . One set came to spy, to learn the land and determine a way to eventually slaughter the people. The other set came representing the king and all his power and his wealth. She chose to side with the spies against her own people. Why did she do it? Taking sides with the spies meant that she was taking sides with God. Perhaps she saw the spies' arrival at her house as her window of escape from her lifestyle. Maybe she had been waiting for someone or something to come along and free her. Certainly, she saw this as an opportunity to save herself and her family from what she believed would be sure defeat and death at the hands of the conquering Israelites.

Even though Rahab worked in one of the vilest of occupations, she still saw the awesomeness of God. Even though she was a social outcast, she still figured out a way to rescue two of God's people. Even though life placed her on the bottom rung of society's ladder, she still declared the goodness of God.

Whatever our circumstance in life, we can still testify about God's magnificence. We should never let the fact that we may not be as prominent as others keep us silent. Rahab seemed to blurt out her belief in God. Apparently, it had been bubbling up in her for quite a while. She could not keep it to herself. There was another who felt something inside and had to share it. He was the prophet Jeremiah who said, "There is in my heart as it were a burning fire, / shut up in my bones, / and I am weary with holding it in, / and I cannot" (Jeremiah 20:9, RSV).

The moment Rahab articulated her belief in God, her entire situation changed. She was no longer just an accomplice of the spies but a believer in God. Her statement on the rooftop transforms her before our eyes. It was time for change in her life. She had had enough. I believe that she understood that she was at the intersection of God's plan and seized the opportunity to believe and serve. God was separating her from her idol-worshiping nation and pressing her close to the Israelites.

Think about your own life in light of Rahab's actions. Are you too at the intersection of God's divine will? Perhaps, like Rahab, God is trying to move you in a new direction.

Reflecting and Recording

Is it time for a change in your life?

Has God ever separated you from a person or group that initially appeared positive but later you found to be negative?

Have you ever shared with someone how you feel about the Lord? What was the person's reaction?

DAY THREE: A BARGAIN IS MADE

Joshua 2:12-14

"Now then, since I have dealt kindly with you, swear to me by the LORD that you in turn will deal kindly with my family. Give me a sign of good faith that you will spare my father and mother, my brothers and sisters, and all who belong to them, and deliver our lives from death." The men said to her, "Our life for yours! If you do not tell this business of ours, then we will deal kindly and faithfully with you when the LORD gives us the land."

Rahab displayed tremendous courage and bravery by aiding and abetting the spies. In effect, she committed treason for the kingdom of God. Yet there was even more to this remarkable woman. She proved that she was also smart. She exacted a promise from the spies that when they returned, along with Joshua and the army, her life and her family's lives would be spared. Single biblical women like Rahab realized that they had to ensure the safety of their own households, or risk becoming beggars.

By saying, "Now then . . . swear to me by the LORD," Rahab indicated that she had staked her life on God just as much as the spies had. They replied, "Our life for yours! If you do not tell this business of ours." The bargain was made and sealed.

In the Old Testament, oaths were binding commitments that could only be made between believers. A nonbeliever had no common basis on which to build such a bond. Rahab further cemented her future to the people of Israel and to God with her oath. This was a faith move. After uttering her rooftop confession, she probably felt close to God, and possibly even sensed God's presence nearby. Moreover, her oath was also a survival move. When the time came, Rahab did not want to be slaughtered with the other residents of Jericho. She recognized that only God could save her. She was right; our God is a safe place and a haven for the persecuted.

We should also note that Rahab could have negotiated the rescue for herself alone, but she did not. She added her family to her agreement with the spies. She wanted all of them to be saved, both physically and spiritually. What a generous spirit she had! Although we do not know what type of relationship she had with her family, we do know that it was a fairly large group, consisting of her mother, father, sisters, brothers, and all who belonged to them (verse 13).

Regardless of the relationship, Rahab felt some level of responsibility for them. Some biblical scholars have suggested that Rahab was a prostitute in order to support her family. They propose that she was a daughter helping her impoverished family survive. Then as now, prostitution is linked to poverty. In biblical times, when a family could not pay their debts, they could either enter debt slavery (see "Week Six: The Widow With the Oil") or prostitution. Unfortunately, desperate families had to make this horrible choice.

Rahab was an intelligent woman who was not afraid to make provisions for the future. She teaches us not to back down or away from making major decisions about our future. Sometimes we shy away from such decisions out of fear, or because we don't want to worry ourselves with details and difficult issues. But like Rahab we can dare to take on what lies ahead, trusting in God's guiding presence.

Reflecting and Recording

Have you thought about your future and made plans for a significant change (for example, a life or career change, a retirement, a funeral)? What role does your faith play in making this decision?

Rahab's actions were motivated, at least in part, by her concern for the lives of her family. Have there been similar situations in your own life when you were motivated to act in order to protect your loved ones? How do such acts of sacrificial love mirror God's love for us?

Think about promises that you have made to others and others have made to you. How does keeping a promise or breaking a promise affect the relationship of the persons involved? Similarly how do promises or pledges made to God either strengthen (if they were kept) or weaken (if they were broken) your relationship with God?

DAY FOUR: THE POWER OF THE RED CORD

Joshua 2:15-21

Then she let them down by a rope through the window, for her house was on the outer side of the city wall and she resided within the wall itself. She said to them, "Go toward the hill country, so that the pursuers may not come upon you. Hide yourselves there three days, until the pursuers have returned; then afterward you may go your way." The men said to her, "We will be released from this oath that you have made us swear to you if we invade the land and you do not tie this crimson cord in the window through which you let us down, and you do not gather into your house your father and mother, your brothers, and all your family. If any of you go out of the doors of your house into the street, they shall be responsible for their own death, and we shall be innocent; but if a hand is laid upon any who are with you in the house, we shall bear the responsibility for their death. But if you tell this business of ours, then we shall be released from this oath that you made us swear to you." She said, "According to your words, so be it." She sent them away and they departed. Then she tied the crimson cord in the window.

The sign that Rahab and her family should be spared death was a red cord or rope that was tied to the window of her home. It was tied to the same window from which she let the spies down when they made their escape.

The window was located on the Jericho wall, facing outward. Only those outside of Jericho could see it. Imagine that red rope blowing in the wind, waiting to be seen by the approaching army. It marked Rahab and her family as believers in an unbelieving world.

The red cord represents a lifeline that carried Rahab away from her scarlet sins and toward God's forgiveness. Her brave and faithful actions on behalf of the spies made the red cord possible. The townspeople of Jericho had no way of seeing the red cord, but I suspect they would have been stunned to learn that the town prostitute had been pardoned by God, used in God's service, and released from the death that would come to everyone else in the city.

The red cord also represented grace, which is God's unmerited favor. Some describe grace as being let off the hook for something one should be in trouble for. Without question, Rahab's reprehensible occupation should have drawn some form of punishment. The religious leaders of her day would probably have had her stoned to death or at least run out of town, but God chose a different route for Rahab and her family.

In a similar way, the Jericho slaughter can be likened to the Egyptian slaughter found in Exodus 12:13. The Lord planned to pass through Egypt and kill all first-born males, except those whose front doors were marked with blood: "The blood shall be a sign for you on the houses where you live: when I see the blood, I will pass over you, and no plague shall destroy you when I strike the land of Egypt" (Exodus 12:13).

Rahab sat in her house and trusted her future to the red cord. She may have had to believe for her entire family as well. I suspect that she was strong enough to do so. Her life and story show us that God is our ultimate judge. As much as we sometimes would like to think differently, we have no control over who gets "red cords" in life. We imagine ourselves capable of making such weighty decisions, but ultimately God makes those life-and-death choices. As Christians, we must avoid the temptation to judge and condemn people that we meet along our faith journey. They may in fact be major players in God's plan.

Rahab and her red cord are also a cause for celebration. We too have access to the red cord, albeit in another form—the life-changing blood of

Jesus Christ. The blood of Jesus washes us clean and restores us. Think for a moment about the Holy Communion ritual, which focuses our attention on the body and blood of Jesus. When I am leading my congregation through the ritual, I savor the words that describe the power of the blood.

"When the supper was over, he took the cup, gave thanks to you, gave it to his disciples, and said: 'Drink from this, all of you; this is my blood of the new covenant, poured out for you and for many for the forgiveness of sins. Do this, as often as you drink it, in remembrance of me' " (*The United Methodist Hymnal,* page 14).

Like Rahab, we too can become clean, restored, and given new life through God's loving, merciful grace.

Reflecting and Recording

Why did God spare Rahab and her family?

Are you marked in some way as a believer? What are the signs that let people know you serve the Lord?

If you were Rahab would you have trusted the red cord to save your life? Why?

DAY FIVE: RESCUED BY GOD'S ARMY

Joshua 6:17, 22-24

The city and all that is in it shall be devoted to the LORD for destruction. Only Rahab the prostitute and all who are with her in her house shall live because she hid the messengers we sent.

Joshua said to the two men who had spied out the land, "Go into the prostitute's house, and bring the woman out of it and all who belong to her, as you swore to her." So the young men who had been spies went in and brought Rahab out, along with her father, her mother, her brothers, and all who belonged to her—they bought all her kindred out—and set them outside the camp of Israel. They burned down the city, and everything in it; only the silver and gold, and the vessels of bronze and iron, they put into the treasury of the house of the LORD.

Horrific, blood-curdling screams filled the air in Jericho when Joshua and his army killed as God had commanded. They were under strict orders to destroy every living thing—men, women, young, old, cattle, sheep, and donkey (Joshua 6:21). Yes, this was severe violence. Yet, we must understand that the God of the Old Testament was a warring God who often led followers into bloody battles. But it is interesting to note that Joshua's army brought down the Jericho wall with no physical effort. The army marched around the wall for six days, and on the seventh day, the priests blew their trumpets; they all gave a shout, and the walls collapsed. Immediately, the word was given to destroy all the inhabitants, except Rahab and her family, because she had hidden Joshua's messengers. The two spies, who initially came to her house, were dispatched to bring Rahab and her family out of Jericho. The city was then burned to the ground.

Rahab's faith was greatly strengthened when the spies kept their word. She had witnessed a miracle from God when the spies came to her house. She had made the oath with them and had tied the red cord to her window as they had instructed her. And the spies remembered to rescue her when the army returned. It must have lifted her low self-esteem to be remembered. As a prostitute, few of the townspeople extended her such courtesy; but God remembered her. She was important in God's eyes. I believe she gained self-respect and dignity from this divine act. Watching Jericho burn may have set a fire in her heart to live for the Lord, because she had been rescued from the destruction.

Years ago when I wrote for a national Christian newspaper, I was assigned a story about a ministry that rehabilitated prostitutes. My assignment was not only to visit the place but also to live among the women to get a real flavor for the ministry. I was a bit hesitant at first. The notion of living among former "ladies of the night" was more than I thought I could handle.

My mind was filled with bothersome stereotypes from the media. Once I arrived, I was ashamed of my previous thoughts. I found a place filled with ordinary women. They looked no different from other women. I interviewed them and learned of the various ways that they had become prostitutes: drug habits, violent homes, sexual abuse. I also learned of how they had moved out of that lifestyle through a relationship with Jesus. Each woman had come to understand that she was special in the eyes of the Master and that she was not forgotten. They, like Rahab, experienced a rescue that made them new women.

I can visualize Rahab watching Jericho burn. It was the end of the only life she had known. The burning ended her ties to her people's pagan gods as well. Out of the ashes of her old life came the beginning of a new one. She was free to start her life again as a believer in God. She may have shed tears of joy and sorrow. It was a pivotal moment in her life. Rahab teaches us that there is power in being remembered by God. Others may forget about us and forsake us, but God never will. We can be sure that whatever promises God makes, God keeps. That is good news.

Reflecting and Recording

How has God ever remembered you?

How has God rescued you?

How did those times make you feel? How did they affect your faith?

DAY SIX: A REVERED WOMAN

Joshua 6:25

*Rahab the prostitute, with her family and all who belonged to her,
Joshua spared. Her family has lived in Israel ever since. For she hid
the messengers whom Joshua sent to spy out Jericho.*

Rahab and her family dwelt among the Israelites, and their lives were
spared. I believe she lived out her life as a celebrated woman among the
Israelites. Few women would have been as bold as she had been. She was
a hero to them. I imagine that this single verse in Joshua barely scratches
the surface of Rahab's stunning new life as a believer. There is so much
more, and it is all a wonderful continuation of the transformation of a
woman with a wicked past. Biblical researchers tell us that one of the two
spies who visited her home, became her husband! His name was Salmon.
Their union produced a son, Boaz, who married Ruth and produced
Obed, the father of Jesse, who was the father of King David. Rahab thus
became a link in the genealogical tree that leads to Jesus Christ! (The
genealogy of Jesus is found in Matthew 1:1.) This is a major place of
honor for her.

There's more. Rahab's selfless actions to save the spies of Joshua lifted
her to the ranks of a revered woman in two additional New Testament
books. The apostle Paul lifts up Rahab as an ideal woman in Hebrews

11:31: "By faith Rahab the prostitute did not perish with those who were disobedient, because she had received the spies in peace." In James 2:25 she is presented as a model for justification of works: "Likewise, was not Rahab the prostitute also justified by works when she welcomed the messengers and sent them out by another road?"

Now that Rahab is spotlighted as a great woman of faith, there is the temptation to go back into the Old Testament and erase her past. Her Old Testament scandalous life seems an inappropriate fit with her New Testament glory. There is the temptation to pretend that she's been a saint all of her life. No way! The ugly, dirty past of Rahab is what makes her a saint. All of us come from something less than perfect. That's what makes us perfect candidates for the love and grace of God. If we were already perfect, what use would we have for God? I don't believe Rahab was ashamed of her past, because it demonstrates the power of God.

These accolades are for the one who was formerly derided by townspeople, judged by her neighbors, and laughed at by other women. With God she experienced a one-way ticket to the top of life. God moved her from the worst to the first. And if God did it for Rahab, God can also do it for you. Rahab shows us that when we connect our lives with God, the sky is the limit. An Old Testament prostitute is redeemed and becomes a New Testament role model. Our God is amazing!

If you've never believed it before, let now be the time. God can do anything in your life but fail.

Reflecting and Recording

What is your reaction to Rahab's elevation?

When we first began this week's reading, did you think that a prostitute could influence your life positively?

Spend time reading and praying over the life of Rahab. Write a few sentences that describe her ability to be transformed. How can you do the same?

DAY SEVEN: GROUP MEETING

Prepare for the meeting by thinking back over your readings and reflections for the week and what you would like to share with the group. You might ponder such questions as these:

♦ As you imagined what it would be like to walk a mile in this woman's shoes, what lessons have you learned from studying the story of this remarkable biblical woman?

♦ How were you strengthened as well as challenged by this story?

♦ What insights have you gained about God from reading about this woman and her relationship with God? How did God act in her life? How has God acted in similar ways in your own life?

♦ What have these stories inspired you to do? How will you put what you have learned into practice?

Pray for the members of your group. Pray that you will be open and receptive to hearing what they have to say as well as what God is saying to you in your time together.

Week Three: Hagar—Moving From Tears to Triumph

Readings for the Week: Genesis 16:1-14

DAY ONE: SITUATIONS BEYOND OUR CONTROL

Genesis 16:1-3

Now Sarai, Abram's wife, bore him no children. She had an Egyptian slave-girl whose name was Hagar, and Sarai said to Abram, "You see that the LORD has prevented me from bearing children; go in to my slave-girl; it may be that I shall obtain children by her." And Abram listened to the voice of Sarai. So, after Abram had lived ten years in the land of Canaan, Sarai, Abram's wife, took Hagar the Egyptian, her slave-girl, and gave her to her husband Abram as a wife.

No one enjoys feeling helpless. You feel helpless when the world seems to be moving in all directions around you, and you cannot control it. You feel helpless when situations occur in your life without permission. You feel helpless when things arise that are beyond your control. You seem to have no influence or input about your situation. I imagine this is probably the way Hagar, the young Egyptian servant to Sarai, felt. Her life was built around pleasing her owners. No one ever asked for her opinions or concerns.

It was common practice in the Old Testament for people of means to own servants. Having numerous servants signified wealth and prosperity. For the most part, the Old Testament offers us insight into the lives of the servant owners. However, this time the story is told from the perspective of the servant.

Modern women live such different lives that it is difficult for us to conceive of life as an indentured servant with no control over our lives or our surroundings. In the daily readings for this week, we encounter an especially challenging section about Hagar's early years. They may be uncomfortable for us to imagine, but Hagar ultimately triumphed with God's help. By exploring Hagar's life and challenges, we too can learn to triumph over adversity. She offers us often painful, yet important lessons on moving from tears to triumph.

Hagar's story takes place in the context of the story of her owners, Sarai and Abram (their names were later changed to Sarah and Abraham). We first meet Sarai and Abram in Genesis 12 when God tells Abram to leave his native land and venture to a new place. In return, God would make him a *great nation,* meaning the father of many. This is a pivotal request, because Abram and Sarai were middle-aged and had no children. They obeyed God; but years later after they had been settled in the new land, Sarai's patience grew thin with her inability to have children. She sought an alternative to giving birth by finding a surrogate mother. It was a Near Eastern tradition for slave women to bear children for their owners when the owner could not. So Sarai offered Hagar to her husband, and the servant woman conceived. Sarai's lack of faith in God's promise changed Hagar's life immensely. If Sarai had believed God's promise that one day she would give birth, Hagar may never have been involved. Sarai shows us how someone else's lapse of faith can create situations beyond our control.

When life appears out of control, we need a faith that will sustain us. Such a faith can help us hold on in situations when there may be no immediate relief to our situation. Faith helps us when our questions go unanswered, when we experience desert times in our faith journey. The readings in this chapter occur while the characters are in the desert. The desert metaphor vividly depicts situations that are beyond our control. Deserts are forbidding and frightening and, on the surface, offer little to sustain life. There is burning sun, whipping sand, and stinging cactus. To survive in the desert, one must dig deep and look beneath the surface.

Desert survival requires resourcefulness and resiliency. We also need the ability to dig deep when we experience desert times in our faith.

Reflecting and Recording

Do you feel any situations are out of your control? How did they get that way? How can you turn them around?

What role does a sustaining faith play in helping you do this?

How do you handle life's unanswered questions?

DAY TWO: MISHANDLED BLESSINGS

Genesis 16:4

*[Abram] went in to Hagar, and she conceived; and when she saw
that she had conceived, she looked with contempt on her mistress.*

What are you doing with the blessings God has given you? Whether it
is a great job, good health, a supportive family, or a reliable car, blessings
should never be used to put others down. In fact, our blessings can be
blessings for others as well. Unfortunately, too often we boast about our
blessings to others in an attempt to make ourselves look and feel good.
This is what Hagar did in today's reading. She mishandled her blessing.

Even in her unstable situation, Hagar was blessed. Hagar's social status
skyrocketed when she became a surrogate mother for Sarai and Abram.
In the Bible, the ability to conceive and bear children was understood to
be a sign of divine favor. Although we know this is not true today, barren
women were believed to be cursed then. So in this light, Hagar was
blessed, while Sarai was cursed. Hagar's pregnancy elevated her above her
slave status. It may have made her feel capable and favored by God, but
it also made her the envy of Sarai. From her new, lofty height, Hagar
looked down on Sarai. No longer the downtrodden humble slave girl, the
pregnant Hagar looked at Sarai with contempt. This is an example of a
mishandled blessing. Hagar's elevation led her to adopt an excluding attitude. As Hagar went up, others went down in her eyes.

Hagar's cruel life to that point likely caused her to be inexperienced and unfamiliar with blessings. She did not know how to receive them. Her behavior illustrates how easy it is to slide into a negative attitude about others when we are "on top." In this instance, Hagar replaced kindness with haughtiness. This behavior enraged Sarai, who in return mistreated Hagar. Sadly, as too often is the case, something positive became negative.

The way that we treat others, especially those who are less fortunate than we, reflects our understanding of what it means to be blessed. Jesus was clear when he said: "From everyone to whom much has been given, much will be required" (Luke 12:48). Many people fail to realize that blessings make us accountable. They raise our profile; and when our status changes, people begin to notice what we do and why we do it.

The blessed are meant to live with humility and service to others. Along with any blessing, comes an obligation. The blessed are to reflect the love of God in their hearts, attitudes, emotions, and actions. The blessed have a special relationship with God. They understand that God is the giver of all blessings. Who are the blessed? All of us have been blessed by God's goodness. We must ensure that we reflect the goodness we have received.

Reflecting and Recording

What are you doing with your blessings? How are you putting them to good use?

Can you find blessings in your life despite the challenges?

What attitudes change when blessings occur?

DAY THREE: YOU CAN RUN BUT YOU CAN'T HIDE

Genesis 16:5-6

*Sarai said to Abram, "May the wrong done to me be on you!
I gave my slave-girl to your embrace, and when she saw that she had
conceived, she looked on me with contempt. May the LORD judge between
you and me!" But Abram said to Sarai, "Your slave-girl is in your power;
do to her as you please." Then Sarai dealt harshly with her,
and she ran away from her.*

A chain reaction of events—Hagar's arrogance and Sarai's response—caused Hagar to flee the home of Sarai and Abram. We have no way of knowing what type of mistreatment Hagar experienced at Sarai's hands. She was a slave, and her life mattered little. Slaves were commonly treated harshly. Regrettably, Sarai was within her rights; and Abram gave her unlimited authority in disciplining Hagar.

Hagar was likely at one of the lowest points of her life. Her tears flowed, and her frustration was high. So she ran away because the pain of being a slave and being mistreated was unbearable. She fled the anguish and suffering she experienced with Sarai and Abram and headed out into the wilderness with nothing but heartache and sorrow. Her decision to run away from her problems is not uncommon. We have all, at some point, run away from a negative situation. Our feelings may have been hurt, or we may have been betrayed. We may have been involved in a quarrel, conflict, or disagreement. We ran because we felt unable to handle the situation or ill-equipped to offer a solution. Fear also causes us to run because it robs us of our confidence in ourselves. Job once spoke of a similar despair. He needed but could not find God. In the midst of his despair, Job says , "If I go forward, he is not there; / or backward, I cannot perceive him; on the left he hides, and I cannot behold him; / I turn to the right, but I cannot see him" (Job 23:8-9).

But there is good news here. Even though Hagar ran away from her problems, she also ran right into God. Actually, she never left God, although her isolation may have made her feel otherwise. She experienced the isolation that comes with tremendous hopelessness and despair. She felt cut off from home and boxed into a dismal situation. She was an Egyptian in a foreign land; and her support, her family and friends, were many miles away. She felt all alone. Such hopelessness can make us feel so low that it seems that God has abandoned us and will never find us.

Like Hagar, when we run from difficult situations, we can run right into God. God is there, even when we are in conflict or confusion, covering us with a blanket of inner peace. We must understand and remember that God is omnipresent, *everywhere,* and omnipotent, *all powerful.* This acknowledgement can prevent us from running away and help us resolve our problems. We are encouraged not to run but instead to rely on God.

Reflecting and Recording

Are there situations or persons that you are running from? List them and ask God to help you confront them.

What do you do when you feel boxed in like Hagar?

How do you believe that an omnipresent God operates?

DAY FOUR: KEEPING YOUR IDENTITY IN THE CRISIS

Genesis 16:7-8

The angel of the LORD found her by a spring of water in the wilderness,
the spring on the way to Shur. And he said, "Hagar, slave-girl of Sarai,
where have you come from and where are you going?"
She said, "I am running away from my mistress Sarai."

"Where have you come from and where are your going?" (verse 8). This is what the angel of the Lord asked Hagar on the wilderness road that led to the town of Shur. The road to Shur was close to Egypt's border, so she was close to home. The angel asked her a soul-searching question. It was more than a logistical question about her travels. This question probed the depth of her being, her emotional, historical, and faith status.

Hagar's response was telling: "I am running away from my mistress Sarai." She was consumed by crisis and could only respond out of her past. The weight of her worries dared her to look ahead, but it was beyond her scope to contemplate a future. Her struggle defined who she was. A crisis can determine our identity or the way we see ourselves, but only if we let it. Unfortunately, we often allow a negative situation to dictate our reaction.

If you were on the run in the wilderness, frantic and desperate, your thinking might be convoluted too. Your answer to the question might be like Hagar's, a reflection of the past. I'd like to ask you the same question: Where have you come from and where are you going? Your answer will say much about you. It reveals your awareness of your present situation, feelings, and spiritual maturity. How do you see yourself, especially in a crisis? When we are in denial, we cannot accurately evaluate our present status.

Another Old Testament woman, Naomi, wanted to change her name to Mara because life became bitter. Her husband and sons had died, and the brunt of those catastrophes made her want to change her name to bitterness (Ruth 1:20-21).

As we see with Hagar and Naomi, a negative past has the power to cripple us if we allow it to. In my work with women who have survived violent encounters, I have found that these women often are bound by their pasts. Their yesterdays were dismal, and they don't know how to release them. Such women tend to color themselves and their world by the events in the painful past.

Great strength is required to break free from the pain of the past. God wants us to look ahead with hope and provides the strength to break free. Faith is a requirement; it means we believe we have a future. Remember this: Our pain is not the end of us. God is not finished, and neither are we. Even though tragedy gives the impression that our lives have come to an end with a period, God shows us it is just a comma or brief pause. God does not want us to be defined by our pain but rather by God's grace and mercy.

Reflecting and Recording

How has pain defined your life?

Where have you been and where are you going?

How has your faith and the assurance of God's loving presence helped you overcome and leave behind painful events of your past?

DAY FIVE: GOING BACK AND STANDING
ON THE PROMISES

Genesis 16:9-12

The angel of the LORD said to her, "Return to your mistress, and submit to her." The angel of the LORD also said to her, "I will so greatly multiply your offspring that they cannot be counted for multitude."
And the angel of the LORD said to her, "Now you have conceived and shall bear a son; / you shall call him Ishmael, / for the LORD has given heed to your affliction. / He shall be a wild ass of a man, / with his hand against everyone, / and everyone's hand against him; / and he shall live at odds with all his kin."

One of the hymns I remember singing as a child was "Standing on the Promises." I liked the hymn because it made perfect sense to me. I knew what it meant to stand on the floor. The floor held me up and did not let me fall. I figured that God's promises were the same. I was right. The promises of God are true. From Genesis to Revelation, we read the accounts of God's faithful relationship with God's people and God's fulfillment of every promise made to them. Unlike human promises, God's promises will not be broken; God will not let us down. These promises serve to keep us standing during the often exhausting journey called life.

God's promises to Hagar turned her away from Egypt and back toward Abram and Sarai's home. The angel of the Lord tells her of God's promise to give her descendants too great in number to count, and of the birth of a son, Ishmael, who would be a free and spirited man. But in return, she had to go back and live with Sarai and Abram.

From our contemporary perspective, this may not make sense. Bear in mind that we do not always understand God's plan for us. God's promises outweighed any problems Hagar faced. Hagar's return to Abram and Sarai was a necessary ingredient in God's plan for all of them. However, this does not mean that we should return to dangerous situations. Rather, the point here is to believe in God's promises and know that God wants the best for us.

Are there promises that God has made to you? Understand that God makes promises out of a longstanding love for you, and that love can carry you through any difficulty and lead you to the fruition of that promise. Don't get discouraged. Don't quit.

I can envision Hagar heading back to the home of Sarai and Abram different than when she left. Her shoulders are thrown back, and there is pep in her step. No, all of her problems are not solved; but God has stepped into her world. Hagar's tears have dried, and she is on the verge of jubilation. God has made her a promise, and she believes God and is energized.

Reflecting and Recording

What has God promised you? How has God been faithful to those promises?

How faithful have you been to the promise?

When you get discouraged, how does God encourage you?

DAY SIX: A GOD WHO SEES ME

Genesis 16:13-14

So she named the LORD who spoke to her, "You are El-roi";
for she said, "Have I really seen God and remained alive after seeing him?"
Therefore the well was called Beer-lahai-roi;
it lies between Kadesh and Bered.

Hagar's moment of triumph came when she realized that God saw her. The great, all-powerful, all-knowing God saw *her.* Suddenly she felt that she mattered. She had value in the sight of the most important One. Her thoughts, ideas, and opinions did matter. After her encounter with the angel, she was certain of two things: that God considered her important, and that she was somebody. She proclaimed, "You are the God who sees me . . . I have now seen the One who sees me" (verse 13, NIV). This was a moment of great celebration.

Hagar's joy at being seen by God must have been similar to the way children bask in the loving attention of their parents or other adults. It's part of our human design to want to be watched by someone older and wiser. Is there a little one in your world who asks you to observe what he is doing? My sons certainly did. "Momma, watch me. Momma, watch me!" they yelled, as they jumped, climbed, ran, or leaped from this to that. Why is that? They want to be observed because it makes them feel important, valued, and loved. Our children feel whole and included when we invest time watching and encouraging them.

In the Book of Psalms the psalmist gives further expression to the joy of being watched over and cared for by God: "I lift up my eyes to the hills— / from where will my help come? / My help comes from the Lord, who made heaven and earth. / He will not let your foot be moved; . . . He who keeps Israel / will neither slumber nor sleep" (Psalm 121:1-4).

Hagar provides us with needed insight to move from trials to triumph. When we believe that God sees us, we know that we are important and not alone. The ability to continue walking away from the pain of our past into a hopeful future can come when we feel God watching and keeping us. Most of all, when God sees us, we don't need to worry about whether any one else does.

God saw Hagar, and her life improved. After she returned to Sarai and Abram, her son Ishmael was born. In Genesis 21:20, we learn that "God was with the boy, and he grew up. . . . He lived in the Desert of Paran; and his mother got a wife for him from the land of Egypt."

Reflecting and Recording

Do you believe that God sees you?

How did a seeing God affect Hagar?

Spend time today reflecting on what it was like to be Hagar. Write a few sentences that describe her journey from tears to triumph and how you can do the same.

DAY SEVEN: GROUP MEETING

Prepare for the meeting by thinking back over your readings and reflections for the week and what you would like to share with the group. You might ponder such questions as these:

♦ As you imagined what it would be like to walk a mile in this woman's shoes, what lessons have you learned from studying the story of this remarkable biblical woman?

♦ How were you strengthened as well as challenged by this story?

♦ What insights have you gained about God from reading about this woman and her relationship with God? How did God act in her life? How has God acted in similar ways in your own life?

♦ What have these stories inspired you to do? How will you put what you have learned into practice?

Pray for the members of your group. Pray that you will be open and receptive to hearing what they have to say as well as what God is saying to you in your time together.

Week Four:
Abigail—Living for God in Spite of the Negative

Readings for the Week: 1 Samuel 25:1-38

DAY ONE: A PRIME EXAMPLE

1 Samuel 25:1-3

Now Samuel died; and all Israel assembled and mourned for him. They buried him at his home in Ramah. Then David got up and went down to the wilderness of Paran. There was a man in Maon, whose property was in Carmel. The man was very rich; he had three thousand sheep and a thousand goats. He was shearing his sheep in Carmel. Now the name of the man was Nabal, and the name of his wife Abigail. The woman was clever and beautiful, but the man was surly and mean; he was a Calebite.

Abigail was a stand-out woman because she lived for God even while living in a negative situation. Living for God means that you exhibit a faithful Christian life, no matter what the circumstance and regardless of whether those around you do so or not. It means living your faith in ways that reflect God. You are not easily swayed by religious fads and trends; your influence comes from above. You don't require pats on the back for your beliefs; your relationship with God is the motivating force that keeps you going.

Abigail's negative situation was that she was married to a man who did not believe in God. His name was Nabal, which means "churlish" and "ill behaved." In fact, it was said that Nabal was a fool. He was a heavy drinker and was known to be disagreeable. In spite of these flaws, Nabal was very wealthy, owning vast amounts of property—three thousand sheep and one thousand goats. In contrast to Nabal, Abigail was a beautiful, intelligent woman. Abigail's name means "good understanding."

The story of this Old Testament woman presents us with the uncomfortable circumstance of an unequally yoked marriage. We see a woman's scramble to survive. Abigail shows us how a wife maintained her faith in God even when her husband had no faith. It's the saga of a beautiful and smart woman who was married to a man who was a fool. Bear in mind that in ancient times, women had little, if any, input into the selection of their husbands. Marriages were negotiated by the men from the groom and bride's families. In all probability, Abigail's beauty was considered an appropriate match for Nabal's money.

Abigail's ability to live for God came to a crescendo when her husband refused to feed David and his small army of six hundred men. (This is the same David who would eventually become king of Jerusalem and become known as a "man after God's own heart.") David and his men had been living on Nabal's land, protecting his shepherds and flocks. When Nabal refused to provide food for David's men, David was insulted and vowed to murder all of the males in Nabal's household. The backdrop of Abigail's story is David's rise from an outlaw on the run from King Saul to king of Jerusalem. If David had not encountered this remarkable woman, his ascent to king might not have happened. Abigail's ability to hold on to her faith in difficult circumstances aided him greatly.

In a similar way, your capacity to maintain your faith in spite of negative situations can help others. God expects us to consistently follow the teachings of the Bible, even though many do not. Disciplined faith is about dedication and steadfastness. The luxurious trimmings that came along with being a rich man's wife did not distract Abigail. It may have been easier and more convenient for her simply to go with the flow and forget about God. She may even have faced the temptation to say to God, "I'll serve you later," or simply to bow down to the idols of wealth. But God gives us the power to press ahead with focus. It is there, if we will recognize and use it. Like Abigail, you too can fight distractions and keep your mind and heart on the Lord.

Reflecting and Recording

When have you been tempted to let go of your faith? How did you handle it?

Have you helped someone else by living for God? What did you do specifically?

How can you help someone who does not believe in God?

DAY TWO: THE IMPORTANCE OF RIGHT NOW

1 Samuel 25:14-18

One of the young men told Abigail, Nabal's wife, "David sent messengers out of the wilderness to salute our master; and he shouted insults at them. Yet the men were very good to us, and we suffered no harm, and we never missed anything when we were in the fields, as long as we were with them; they were a wall to us both by night and by day, all the while we were with them keeping the sheep. Now therefore know this and consider what you should do; for evil has been decided against our master and against all his house; he is so ill-natured that no one can speak to him." Then Abigail hurried and took two hundred loaves, two skins of wine, five sheep ready dressed, five measures of parched grain, one hundred clusters of raisins, and two hundred cakes of figs.

Abigail had to move with haste. Her entire family was about to be murdered as a result of Nabal's behavior. He had committed two potentially deadly errors. He slurred David by calling him a runaway slave and refused to feed David's men. Biblical customs relied heavily on a spirit of hospitality to travelers. It was tradition to provide food and drink to those passing through, or in David's case, to those who had protected one's workers. In retaliation, David reacted harshly and planned a mass murder. As soon as a servant informed Abigail of David's plan, she lost no time in creating a solution.

Watch the way Abigail calmly set herself in motion. On short notice, she assembled and sent a banquet of bread, wine, sheep, grain, and cakes for David and his men. She recognized that the situation was severe and that immediate action was required. Abigail also had a healthy respect for time. She demonstrated the way to decisively use the time available in a dire situation. Moreover, she was able to bypass the panic that too often paralyzes us during a crisis.

She did not tell her husband what she was doing. This was a controversial decision, both then and now. She believed that telling him would slow down what needed to be done in haste. Verse 17 says of Nabal, "He is so ill-natured that no one can speak to him." Rather than fretting about what to do, she took action. Abigail moved with swiftness and decisiveness because she believed her actions could make a difference. She also believed that God was with her.

We also have the power of *right now* in our lives. Each day we have twenty-four hours at our disposal. The way that we use the time available to us indicates how we view urgency and ourselves. On one hand, we may be accustomed to someone else stepping in and fighting our battles. Or we may hope that the problem goes away, so we deny its seriousness. The ability to bravely face bad news is a skill we can all use. Someday we will encounter bad news and will need to respond independently.

There may be areas of your life that cry out for immediate action like Abigail's. Procrastination may be holding you back. Waiting or sitting around when we need to act is simply a way of avoiding the task at hand. People procrastinate for a number of reasons—because they have negative beliefs about themselves, they fear failure; or they feel overwhelmed by the situation. Procrastination is also a faith issue. We simply don't have the confidence that God will help us solve our problems.

Abigail seized the moment and moved ahead. She did not hesitate or wait. If she had paused for a second, history may have been altered. Your actions now may change the future. The clock is ticking. *Now* is in your hands.

Reflecting and Recording

What do you do when you hear that bad news is coming your way?

Are you a procrastinator? If so what can you do to change that?

Do you think Hannah's decision not to tell Nabal what she was doing was wise? Why or why not?

DAY THREE: SEEKING FORGIVENESS

1 Samuel 25:23-25

When Abigail saw David, she hurried and alighted from the donkey, and fell before David on her face, bowing to the ground. She fell at his feet and said, "Upon me alone, my lord, be the guilt; please let your servant speak in your ears, and hear the words of your servant. My lord, do not take seriously this ill-natured fellow, Nabal; for as his name is, so is he; Nabal is his name, and folly is with him; but I, your servant, did not see the young men of my lord, whom you sent.

Riding her donkey into the mountain ravine, Abigail may have prayed and sang to calm herself in the midst of a dangerous mission. Who knew that living for God could lead to a life or death situation? Abigail, though, was a bold woman, who did something unheard of in her day. She took matters into her own hands. She attempted to save her entire household from death, and she decided to do it alone. Flanked by his army, David angrily vowed death at the top of his lungs, as he rode toward her in the same mountain ravine. If this were a suspense-filled, action-packed movie, the next scene would be filled with screams and bloodshed. However, God is the director of this story; so instead of bloodshed there was bold witness. Abigail dismounted; and in an act of obeisance, she bowed her face to the ground at David's feet. This posture symbolized humility and regret. She apologized for the insult, accepted the blame for the problem, and asked that Nabal be overlooked due to his foolish nature.

It takes a special person to apologize for someone else's wrongdoing. Abigail was that special person. She was living for God and did not find it difficult to humble herself. Her faith comforted and guided her. Abigail was able to look ahead and weigh the outcomes. She saw the consequences of what might or might not happen and swept aside her pride. Yes, she was a wealthy woman, and David was an outlaw on the run, but Abigail still apologized. She moved aside her anger with her husband, too. None of these unfortunate events would have occurred if her husband had honored the initial request. But Abigail's displeasure with Nabal did not prevent her from doing what needed to be done.

Like Abigail, we need to take action to reconcile ourselves to those whom we have offended. And we need to address these situations immediately, lest they fester. We should seek forgiveness by verbally acknowledging the mistake or harm done, expressing our sorrow for the mistake, and making amends. Abigail teaches us about the power of an apology. We live in a materialistic world where people often believe that a gift can repair all offenses. A gift can help, but it cannot replace an apology. Abigail brought gifts, but her words were offered before the gifts. Her example teaches us to be bold enough to take the first step, to seek out the person who is offended. By seeking them out, they see our sincerity and effort to make amends. In addition, Abigail teaches us to demonstrate humility. Although we don't have to bow down at a person's feet, we can show humility through our speech, tone, attitude, and posture. In 2 Chronicles 7:14 we are given a model for seeking forgiveness: "If my people who are called by my name humble themselves, pray, seek my face, and turn from their wicked ways, then I will hear from heaven, and will forgive their sin and heal their land."

Seeking forgiveness is never to be taken lightly, but we can follow Abigail's lead. She shows us that as believers we must sometimes be prepared to go all the way for God.

Reflecting and Recording

Who needs an apology from you?

What will it require of you to offer an apology?

Why is humility so difficult?

DAY FOUR: BOLDNESS THAT COMES FROM GOD

1 Samuel 25:26-31

*Now then, my lord, as the LORD lives, and as you yourself live,
since the LORD has restrained you from bloodguilt and from taking
vengeance with your own hand, now let your enemies and those who seek
to do evil to my lord be like Nabal. And now let this present that your servant
has brought to my lord be given to the young men who follow my lord.
Please forgive the trespass of your servant; for the LORD will certainly make
my lord a sure house, because my lord is fighting the battles of the LORD;
and evil shall not be found in you so long as you live. If anyone should rise up
to pursue you and to seek your life, the life of my lord shall be bound
in the bundle of the living under the care of the LORD your God;
but the lives of your enemies he shall sling out as from the hollow of a sling.
When the LORD has done to my lord according to all the good
that he has spoken concerning you, and has appointed you prince over Israel,
my lord shall have no cause of grief, or pangs of conscience, for having shed
blood without cause or for having saved himself. And when the LORD
has dealt well with my lord, then remember your servant.*

"The LORD lives" (verse 26), Abigail proclaimed. She based her actions
on the truth that God was a living being, who was alive in her world. She
was emboldened because of this belief.

Abigail spoke words that were a soothing balm to the seething David. Her boldness originated from the power of God. No other source could have equipped her so exceedingly. She interpreted David's past by assuring him that God was on his side, and that if his enemies (such as King Saul) rose against him, God would protect his life with care. She spoke futuristically of the day when David would be appointed the ruler of Israel. She also shrewdly petitioned him to remember her when all of his blessings came to fruition.

Abigail's capacity to speak a godly word at just the right time is further evidence of how she lived for God. Although her spouse had no interest in God, she did. Refusing to share his godless lifestyle, she reaped the reward of having a personal relationship with God. Her words to David came forth with the conviction of a woman whose faith had carried her through the storms of life. She did not parrot what she heard others say. The authority Abigail displayed in today's readings has led many to conclude that she was sent to David as a prophetic agent or vessel to usher him into his destiny. Her boldness helped to shape his future.

God wants to use us in similar ways. Your willingness is enough. Shyness or introversion can be overcome. Fear and fright can be abandoned. God is the great transformer and will provide the necessary intensity and passion.

However, we must also do our part by studying and learning the Bible and all we can about God. We can also do our part by telling the world about God's goodness. Our relationship with God is exactly what someone needs to hear. Perhaps it's a co-worker, someone who rides the bus with you, or a family member. Don't worry about being perfect; just let God use you.

Remember that God transformed a host of people in the Scriptures from cowardly to brave. Persons such as Moses, Isaiah, and Jeremiah come to mind. Each of them, like Abigail, had not planned on being heroes; but God had other plans.

In this passage, we see that living for God is akin to being a polished and poised warrior of words. We too can become agile fighters adapting quickly to our ever-changing surroundings. Like Abigail, we can think on our feet and gauge situations fast. As we blend the words of the Lord into our conversations with others, we can affect the world. This world of ours needs to know this. We must share the life-changing message of God's love and protection with others.

Reflecting and Recording

Can you be as bold as Abigail? What situation would prompt it?

Have there been situations where you hesitated to act, whether it was out of fear or procrastination or lack of self-confidence? How did your inaction or hesitation affect the situation? How might you have handled things more effectively?

How does your faith affect your level of self-confidence and boldness? How does your assurance of God's love and grace enable you to be bold?

DAY FIVE: BEING FORGIVEN

1 Samuel 25:32-35

David said to Abigail, "Blessed be the LORD, the God of Israel, who sent you to meet me today! Blessed be your good sense, and blessed be you, who have kept me today from bloodguilt and from avenging myself by my own hand! For as surely as the LORD the God of Israel lives, who has restrained me from hurting you, unless you had hurried and come to meet me, truly by morning there would not have been left to Nabal so much as one male." Then David received from her hand what she had brought him; he said to her, "Go up to your house in peace; see, I have heeded your voice, and I have granted your petition."

David's heart was softened, and he forgave Nabal's insult. He accepted Abigail's gift of food and said, "Go up to your house in peace; see I have heeded your voice" (verse 35). He sent her home with the same blessings that he initially attempted to give to Nabal. He realized that her efforts kept him from bloodguilt, from avenging himself rather than leaving vengeance to God. David celebrated Abigail's bold and brave efforts with a series of blessings. There were three of them, and they were intended to heap goodness on her life. Throughout the Bible, people constantly blessed each other and blessed the Lord. It was a divine wish, a positive sendoff, a hope for happiness. This was an incredible moment for Abigail and David. Forgiveness saturated the air. Do you remember how it feels to be forgiven? It is one of the best experiences in life. It's as if a weight has been lifted off your chest, or as if perennial dark clouds give way to the sun. In Abigail's case, though, the stakes were higher. It meant that her family would not be slaughtered. Abigail's acceptance of David's forgiveness is also important. Many of us find it challenging to allow ourselves to be forgiven.

Most of us have been on both sides of this situation: We have been the one seeking forgiveness and the one doing the forgiving. We know how Abigail and David felt. There is joy, relief, and peace. When we forgive, we stop carrying around the pain of the offense. However, as long as we carry that pain, we rehash and rehearse the situation that caused it in the first place. It is as if we place ourselves in a jar of bitter, sour marinade. Forgiveness cracks the jar open and allows fresh, freeing air to come inside. Unfortunately, some people have a hard time with forgiveness. They think that it offers the offender an easy way out, and that the offense is legitimated. Forgiveness never affirms the wrong; rather it indicates that the burden has been carried around long enough. Forgiveness says it is time to move on with life. Forgiveness does not necessarily erase the pain; sometimes the wound is so deep that time is required to heal. However, forgiveness can begin the process.

All of us have encountered people—perhaps a few who even sit in the pews alongside us—who are suffering from anger and bitterness because they have not offered or accepted forgiveness. On the surface they seem fine, yet they are difficult to get along with. Deep inside they are holding on to something that happened years ago. There was a woman in my church who I will always remember because of the hostile attitude and menacing glares she directed at her fellow church members, even though they were not the cause of her feelings. Her anger stemmed from her father's deeds that had occurred long ago. People cringed when they saw her and assumed that she was angry with them. Yet, her anger was not with them but was instead about the fact that she had not let go of her anger and hurt; she had not forgiven her father.

Jesus often spoke about the importance of forgiving others, which is tied to God's willingness to forgive us. In Luke 11:4 he said: "Forgive us our sins, / for we ourselves forgive everyone indebted to us." If David had refused to accept Abigail's apology and slaughtered her household, he might never have become one of Israel's greatest kings. Without forgiveness, you too may miss the blessings that God has in store for you.

Reflecting and Recording

How do you think Abigail was able to forgive Nabal?

Are there persons whom you should forgive? What steps can you take toward letting go of your hurt and anger?

Why does God combine forgiveness of us with our forgiveness of others?

DAY SIX: HOMECOMING

1 Samuel 25:36-38

Abigail came to Nabal; he was holding a feast in his house, like the feast of a king. Nabal's heart was merry within him, for he was very drunk; so she told him nothing at all until the morning light. In the morning, when the wine had gone out of Nabal, his wife told him these things, and his heart died within him; he became like a stone. About ten days later the LORD struck Nabal, and he died.

Doing the right thing is always the correct choice. For example, living for God means taking the high road in all situations. After her encounter with David, Abigail returned home as the dutiful wife. She was, however, also a victorious wife by staying the hand of death. Yet she did not gloat or appear arrogant. This victor returned home minus the victory song. To her surprise, Nabal had thrown himself a party. He seemed oblivious to what had occurred in the mountain ravine. Or perhaps he was aware and chose to drown his shame in alcohol. Either way, he did not thank her. Abigail risked her life to save his, and yet he showed her no appreciation. If she had not been living for God, this oversight would have hurt deeply. It did not, because she knew that God was in control.

From this point Abigail's life moved like a roller coaster, quickly and unpredictably. The morning after meeting David, she informed Nabal of her activities; the news turned him to stone. Ten days later, God struck

Nabal, and he died. When David received word of Nabal's death, he quickly wooed and married Abigail. The ending of this story has twists and turns that no one could predict. Abigail's victory hardened her husband instead of pleasing him. This shows us that God's triumph is often not appreciated or valued by non-believers. The victory is valid nonetheless.

Some condemn Abigail for her handling of the news to Nabal, but she made the best of a bad situation. Women did not have the upper hand in any situation at that time. God dealt with Nabal, on God's terms. Others have criticized Abigail's swift marriage to David. However, we must bear in mind though that a widow was a helpless, defenseless woman. Biblical women needed a man—a father, son, husband, or brother—to survive.

What we can learn from this brave woman is how to maintain poise and composure in any situation. Abigail kept her head up, even in the storm; and she believed that God would be faithful. I'm glad that she was such a strong witness. The fact that she did not lose her temper with Nabal speaks highly of her. Otherwise, her witness may have been compromised.

Abigail became the second wife of David. God took care of Abigail, just as God will also take care of us. She bore children with David. Yet, when we read of the episode of David's affair with Bathsheba, we can guess that even this marriage was not perfect. What marriage is? God never promised ease but faithfulness. With God's help, though, we can be certain that Abigail handled whatever situation came her way. By following her example of living faithfully, we can as well.

Reflecting and Recording

What impresses you most about Abigail?

How has your faith in God sustained you through difficult times?

Spend time today reflecting and praying about the life of Abigail. What was it like to live for God despite negative situations? Write a few sentences that describe how you can live for God like Abigail did.

DAY SEVEN: GROUP MEETING

Prepare for the meeting by thinking back over your readings and reflections for the week and what you would like to share with the group. You might ponder such questions as these:

♦ As you imagined what it would be like to walk a mile in this woman's shoes, what lessons have you learned from studying the story of this remarkable biblical woman?

♦ How were you strengthened as well as challenged by this story?

♦ What insights have you gained about God from reading about this woman and her relationship with God? How did God act in her life? How has God acted in similar ways in your own life?

♦ What have these stories inspired you to do? How will you put what you have learned into practice?

Pray for the members of your group. Pray that you will be open and receptive to hearing what they have to say as well as what God is saying to you in your time together.

Week Five:
Hannah—Loving God Despite the Pain

Readings for the Week: 1 Samuel 1:1-28

DAY ONE: HURTING BUT STILL TRUSTING GOD

1 Samuel 1:1-3

*There was a certain man of Ramathaim, a Zuphite from the hill country
of Ephraim, whose name was Elkanah son of Jeroham son of Elihu
son of Tohu son of Zuph, an Ephraimite. He had two wives; the name
of the one was Hannah, and the name of the other Peninnah.
Peninnah had children, but Hannah had no children.
Now this man used to go up year by year from his town to worship
and to sacrifice to the LORD of hosts at Shiloh, where the two sons of Eli,
Hophni and Phinehas, were priests of the LORD.*

"The LORD had closed her womb" (verse 5). These five solemn words
sound more like an ending than a beginning, but for Hannah they were
a starting point for loving God. Hannah's womb was closed, but she
remained open and available to God. This is her lesson to us.

Hannah was, no doubt, haunted by her closed womb, particularly in
a society that devalued infertile women. Childlessness was considered a
curse; and she felt cursed above all. Hannah was a long-suffering woman,
who felt insecure and unworthy. Her pain was not implied; it was real.
We can easily feel her anguish and hear her cries as we read this text. She
was an expressive biblical woman. We don't have to guess what was on

her mind. She released what she felt. Yet she trusted God. She was in pain, but she did not turn away from God. She did not investigate alternatives or look for a way to fix her infertility as Sarai did (Genesis 16:1-3).

Hannah's barrenness drove her into an intense relationship with God that is worth exploring. The backdrop of her story is her family's annual journey to Shiloh for sacrifice in the temple. The trip probably produced great anxiety for her because it magnified her isolation as a woman who could not bear children. The crowds, the religious ceremonies, the children of other mothers may have saddened her. In the midst of this chaos though, she faithfully kept her hand in God's. Hannah demonstrates that ongoing communication with God will sustain us in difficult times.

In our pain, we might be tempted to put God on the back burner or, even worse, desert God altogether When we are hurting, the pain can make us turn away rather than toward God. Pain by its very nature captures our attention. If we slice our flesh with the sharp edge of a crisp piece of paper, the pronounced sting of the cut draws our attention to the bleeding finger. Pain makes us focus on the problem, but faith steps in to remind us that pain is only temporary.

After we recognize the source of our pain, we must, however, refocus on God, the source of the solution. The disciples also chose to focus only on their pain when a storm rapidly approached their small boat. They panicked and cried out to Jesus for help: "Do you not care if we are perishing?" Jesus rebuked the waves and calmed the seas with the words, "Peace! Be still!" Then Jesus asked the disciples, "Have you still no faith?" (Mark 4:37). Although the disciples lost their focus in a time of crisis, we, like Hannah, can choose to stay focused on God whatever the situation.

Reflecting and Recording

Can you still trust God in the midst of pain? How do you know? Remember a difficult time when you stayed focused on God. What made the difference?

Is God present when you are in pain? Why do we seem to forget that?

How was Hannah able to love God still even though her womb was closed? In a similar situation, could you?

DAY TWO: I LOVE YOU JUST THE WAY YOU ARE

1 Samuel 1:4-5, 8

*On the day when Elkanah sacrificed, he would give portions to his wife
Peninnah and to all her sons and daughters; but to Hannah he gave
a double portion, because he loved her, though the LORD had closed her
womb. . . . Her husband Elkanah said to her, "Hannah, why do you weep?
Why do you not eat? Why is your heart sad?
Am I not more to you than ten sons?"*

Hannah's husband, Elkanah, loved her dearly, even though she was
unable to have children. Elkanah actually had two wives, Hannah and
Peninnah. Polygamy was an accepted practice with biblical figures; Jacob
and David also had multiple wives. But Hannah was the favored wife.
At Shiloh Elkanah gave Hannah a double portion of the meat from the
sacrifice, though she was due only a single portion because she had no
children. Elkanah was also aware of her sorrows. While at Shiloh,
Elkanah noted Hannah's tears and spoke softly to her regarding her lost
appetite and downcast spirit. He asked, "Am I not more to you than ten
sons?" (verse 8). This was his attempt to cheer her and reassure her of his
devotion.

Elkanah was a caring, compassionate husband. We know that he was a
devout Jew, since he observed the annual festivals and made sacrifices at
the temple. Elkanah did what he could to offer support to his hurting

wife. He offered her both the tangible meat and the intangible emotional support. This text offers a rare glimpse into an intimate, caring moment between a biblical husband and wife. A supportive spouse aids the weary spirit that is attempting to hold on to a love for God in difficult times. Hannah was loved just the way she was. Elkanah's love for Hannah ran counter to the emphasis and value that their society placed on childbearing. This was powerful love.

Hannah teaches us the importance of allowing someone to love us. This may sound elementary or simplistic, but accepting love from another is not an automatic response, particularly if we are in agony. We may feel we don't have the time, space, or even the right to be loved. The intensity of Hannah's suffering had the power to demean her soul and create a pervasive sense of worthlessness. I have seen hurting people push away attempts by others to comfort them. They resist love because their discomfort is so intense. They fear that if they accept the affection, they would only receive more pain.

Never allow your pain to shut you off from tenderness offered by others. The support we receive from other people—spouses, parents, children, or church members—may be exactly what God has prescribed to carry us through desolate times. God reaches out to us in many ways, often through the small acts of kindness from others. We must stay open and receptive to God's blessings.

The most important message here is that God loves us just the way we are. We don't have to be ashamed of who we are because God created us. God has been in love with us from our beginning. Reflect on the words found in Jeremiah 1:5: "Before I formed you in the womb I knew you, / and before you were born I consecrated you."

Reflecting and Recording

What role did Elkanah's love play in Hannah's ability to love God in the midst of her pain?

Have you resisted love because of your pain? How can you become more open to this love?

Why is accepting love from another person sometimes difficult?

DAY THREE: LOVING GOD IN SPITE
OF JEALOUSY AND ENVY

1 Samuel 1:6-8

*Her rival used to provoke her severely, to irritate her, because the L*ORD
*had closed her womb. So it went on year by year; as often as she went up
to the house of the L*ORD*, she used to provoke her.
Therefore Hannah wept and would not eat. Her husband Elkanah
said to her, "Hannah, why do you weep? Why do you not eat?
Why is your heart sad? Am I not more to you than ten sons?"*

A household with one husband and two wives is beyond our imagina-
tion. From our modern-day vantage point this household arrangement
makes no sense. Peninnah, Elkanah's other wife, taunted Hannah constantly. They were rivals in the cultural contest for who can give birth to
the most children. The tally was summed up in the sentence, "Peninnah
had children, but Hannah had no children" (verse 2). As you might
expect, there was ongoing tension. The text tells us that Hannah's rival
"used to provoke her severely, to irritate her" (verse 6). We can easily
imagine the malicious comments, name calling, insults, and put downs
that she endured.

Their names aptly described them. *Hannah* means "charming" and
"attractive," while *Peninnah* means "fertile" or "prolific." The root of the

tension was Peninnah's jealousy. She was jealous of Elkanah's love for Hannah. However, Hannah refused to retaliate. She may not have struck back or sought revenge because she had a more pressing agenda. She may have realized that retaliating would not alter her infertility. It would be a waste of energy that could instead be devoted to loving God.

I believe it was Hannah's love for God that held her anger back. Her devotion to God's teachings kept her from responding negatively. As the favored wife, she had every right to ask her husband to intervene. Instead, Hannah waited on a higher power to do more than intervene. She knew that God was powerful enough to completely rearrange the scene. Like Hannah, we too must believe that God can and will rearrange our trying scenes.

All of us have someone like Peninnah in our lives, people who thrive on seeing us unhappy or suffering. The plain truth is that Peninnah was a bully. Bullies are people who try to control others through fear and anger. They belittle and torment others incessantly. As a result, their victims feel shame, embarrassment, and fear. Sometimes, their health declines, or they become depressed. Peninah's bullying may also have been the reason that Hannah wept so and could not eat.

Perhaps you encountered bullies on the playground during your childhood. Well, they are still around. We find them in our offices and even in our churches. Bullies can distract us from our goals by diverting our focus. I was bullied by a girl classmate in elementary school. It makes little sense now; but back then, she was mean and hurt my feelings with her cruel words. Every day my stomach knotted up on the playground when I saw her coming toward me. I did not know what to do. Eventually, I told a teacher who intervened.

Although God ultimately handles all bullies, we must let the bullies we encounter know that their actions will not be tolerated. We serve a God who does not accept the mistreatment of God's people. In Isaiah 54:17, God spoke passionately about protecting God's own: "No weapon that is fashioned against you shall prosper / and you shall confute every tongue that rises against you in judgment."

Reflecting and Recording

Are there bullies in your life? How do you handle them? Would following Hannah's example work for you?

How do you deal with jealous people, especially those in the church?

How can you love God and protect yourself at the same time? In what ways does God provide protection for you?

DAY FOUR: TAKE IT TO THE LORD

1 Samuel 1:9-11

After they had eaten and drunk at Shiloh, Hannah rose and presented herself before the LORD. Now Eli the priest was sitting on the seat beside the doorpost of the temple of the LORD. She was deeply distressed and prayed to the LORD, and wept bitterly. She made this vow: "O LORD of hosts, if only you will look on the misery of your servant, and remember me, and not forget your servant, but will give to your servant a male child, then I will set him before you as a nazirite until the day of his death. He shall drink neither wine nor intoxicants, and no razor shall touch his head."

After the family concluded their dinner at Shiloh, Hannah abruptly rose and departed. She could not take the pain anymore. Her endurance was spent. She was tired of weary, tear-filled, red eyes. She ran into the temple past Eli, the elderly priest, who sat by the front door. Hannah could have run to a number of places to seek relief, but tellingly she ran to God's house. God's house was a place of safety and refuge. The ark of God was located in the temple at Shiloh, making it even more special. She believed that she could find solace there. Pouring out her concerns before the Lord, she prayed, and she cried. Imagine her there with arms flailing, body shivering, head rocking to and fro, and unchecked tears streaming down her face. She prayed with power and abandon.

Then she made a vow to God. Vows were made between people and between a person and God, as a means of binding one to a specific promise. Hannah vowed that if she gave birth to a male child, she would give him back to God. She vowed to raise him as a member of the nazarites, a religious community known never to cut their hair or indulge in strong drink. Hannah meant business. She was serious about her situation.

Hannah points out for us the path each of us can take out of pain—to go deeper and stronger into our connection with God. Most of all, Hannah's example encourages us not to give up. Her prayers opened the door to God, and her vow cemented her connection with God. Hannah had unshakable confidence, even when there was no visible reason to have any. Sheer faith was her guide. She knew instinctively that no one on earth could do what the Lord can do. I particularly admire her steadfastness, the way she never wavered.

When our problems become serious, we search for solutions. Daytime talk shows are popular places where people turn for guidance. Hour after hour, viewers are presented with solutions galore. While the television experts have merit, they must never be our ultimate source. It is easy to hear their advice and then consider the matter resolved. However, our problems are not settled until we take them to God. Hannah shows us the importance of turning to God with our problems. As believers, it is fine to have friends and confidents; but God is the ultimate source for problem solving: "Cast all your anxiety on him, because he cares for you" (1 Peter 5:7).

Prayer is a reliable path to God. At St. Paul United Methodist Church, where I am pastor, we have altar call every Sunday; and it is a highlight of the service. Each Sunday, people seem to anticipate this moment. Worshipers come to the front of the sanctuary, kneel on pillows surrounding a wooden, circular rail, and pour out their hearts to God. The aisle clogs with worshipers patiently waiting their turn at the altar. No issues are too small for God, and kneeling before the altar is a privilege. Once they kneel, people seem to forget about everybody else. They enter their own private meeting space with the Almighty. Some are silent and motionless. Others weep, lift their hands, and some shout, "Hallelujah!"

Like Hannah, they pray with abandon. They don't focus on what others think, but rather on what God thinks.

Reflecting and Recording

Do you, like Hannah, see the church as a refuge? What happens there for you?

Can you pray your way through trouble?

Have you made a vow to God? Have you kept it? If not, what are the reasons you have failed to do so?

DAY FIVE: YOU WILL BE MISUNDERSTOOD —EVEN IN CHURCH

1 Samuel 1:12-18

*As she continued praying before the LORD, Eli observed her mouth.
Hannah was praying silently; only her lips moved, but her voice
was not heard; therefore Eli thought she was drunk.So Eli said to her, "How
long will you make a drunken spectacle of yourself? Put away your wine."
But Hannah answered, "No, my lord, I am a woman deeply troubled;
I have drunk neither wine nor strong drink, but I have been pouring out
my soul before the LORD. Do not regard your servant as a worthless woman,
for I have been speaking out of my great anxiety and vexation all this time."
Then Eli answered, "Go in peace; the God of Israel grant the petition you
have made to him." And she said, "Let your servant find favor in your sight."
Then the woman went to her quarters, ate and drank with her husband,
and her countenance was sad no longer.*

Misunderstandings at church occur despite our best intentions. Eli, the priest, intensely watched Hannah's feverish prayers. Perhaps few came to Shiloh to pray with such passion or desperation. Hannah prayed in her heart. Her lips moved, but no sound came forth. But Eli misinterpreted her actions, accusing her of being drunk and ordering her to put away her wine. Hannah defended herself saying, "I am a woman deeply troubled;

I have drunk neither wine nor strong drink, . . . I have been speaking out of my great anxiety and vexation" (verses 15-16). Once Eli understood her situation, he promised that God would honor her request, without even knowing what it was! He did not need to know, because Eli knew two things: (1) that God is able and (2) that Hannah was utterly devoted to God. Eli saw her love, respected her, and honored her request. Hannah departed expecting something good from God. She sensed that something had changed: "Hannah ate and drank with her husband, and her countenance was sad no longer" (verse 18).

Hannah's defense of herself made the difference in her quest for favor. She was not pouring wine but rather pouring out her heart to God. Her ability to defend herself gained her access to the ear of God. If she had remained timid, she might not have changed Eli's perception of her. Hannah prayed to God, but human error threatened to derail her passageway. She came to Shiloh for a blessing from God and was determined that no misunderstanding would deter it.

Hannah's story shows us that even when we are most sincere, we may be misunderstood. People may not understand our motives, but we can remain undeterred. Our love for God shouldn't allow us to keep quiet regarding our motives. Conversely, we must avoid making snap judgments about people and situations at church and elsewhere. Until we have walked a mile in their shoes, we don't know what others may be going through.

Have you ever been misunderstood at church? It may have happened when you served on a committee, or drove into the parking lot, or even when you received Communion. We are all imperfect people who make mistakes, so it is easy to identify with how Hannah must have felt. The improper response would have been anger or offense. Too many Christians sit at home refusing to return to church because they have been offended by something that has happened. These negative responses to past hurts, whether intended or accidental, do not help the body of believers. They simply keep us separated and angry with each other.

I once had a major misunderstanding while guest preaching at a church. I was not aware of it, but the church had an active ministry to the deaf and hard-of-hearing. In fact, directly beside me, sat a person with hearing who was signing my sermons for someone who could hear only slightly. These two people apparently were enjoying the sermon and made quite a commotion. But I did not understand. I thought they were being disrespectful and became angry—even as I preached. The louder I raised my voice to cover theirs, the louder they became. Afterwards, I complained to the host pastor, who explained what was happening. I was ashamed because I had misunderstood what was happening.

Like Hannah, when a misunderstanding occurs, we can rise above feeling slighted. Those around us will honor and respect us if we are able to articulate our positions clearly. Hannah did just that, and Eli relented and blessed her request.

Reflecting and Recording

Have past misunderstandings stood in your way? Have you resolved them?

Are there situations in your life when you have made a snap judgment about a situation or someone and therefore likely misunderstood the situation? Consider ways that you can make amends and also avoid such misunderstandings in the future.

Are you easily offended? If so, ask for God's help with that issue.

DAY SIX: FAITHFUL TO GOD'S VOW

1 Samuel 1:19-28

They rose early in the morning and worshiped before the LORD;
then they went back to their house at Ramah. Elkanah knew his wife Hannah,
and the LORD remembered her. In due time Hannah conceived and bore a son.
She named him Samuel, for she said, "I have asked him of the LORD."
The man Elkanah and all his household went up to offer to the LORD
the yearly sacrifice, and to pay his vow. But Hannah did not go up,
for she said to her husband, "As soon as the child is weaned, I will bring him,
that he may appear in the presence of the LORD, and remain there forever;
I will offer him as a nazirite for all time." Her husband Elkanah said to her,
"Do what seems best to you, wait until you have weaned him;
only—may the LORD establish his word." So the woman remained
and nursed her son, until she weaned him. When she had weaned him,
she took him up with her, along with a three-year-old bull, an ephah of flour,
and a skin of wine. She brought him to the house of the LORD at Shiloh;
and the child was young. Then they slaughtered the bull, and they brought
the child to Eli. And she said, "Oh, my lord! As you live, my lord,
I am the woman who was standing here in your presence, praying to the
LORD. For this child I prayed; and the LORD has granted me the petition
that I made to him. Therefore I have lent him to the LORD; as long
as he lives, he is given to the LORD." She left him there for the LORD.

Hannah continued to love God, this time in new and exciting ways. God had heard her prayers. She was a different woman after leaving Shiloh. The family returned to their home in Ramah, where she conceived and gave birth to a son whom she named Samuel, which means "I have asked him of the Lord." When Samuel was weaned, she took him to the temple and gave him back to Eli, the priest who had initially blessed her. She was steadfast to her vow because God had been faithful. She was loyal to a God who was trustworthy. Hannah's story should not imply that every woman who experiences infertility will become pregnant. That would be an unfair understanding of faithfulness and blessings. Rather, her story confirms our ability to love God in all circumstances and gratefully receive the blessings that God offers.

I believe that Hannah experienced a different type of pain at this point in the text. Cradling the baby she had so desperately wanted, she prepared to give him back to God. Once she took the boy to Eli, she would no longer have daily contact with him. Eli and the temple priests would become his new family. As a Nazarite, her son would be different and set apart from others. It is difficult to fathom how a new mother must feel who knows she must relinquish her child. There must have been great sorrow and anxiety. Yet Hannah's love for God helped her handle this struggle too, and even find excitement in continuing to show her love in new ways.

She could have changed her mind and refused to honor her vow to God. Or she could have delayed giving the boy to Eli for years. Hannah did neither; once the child was weaned, she took him to Shiloh. She took the baby to the temple in an attitude of gratitude and praise. She took with her a container of flour, wine, and a three-year-old bull. These were expensive sacrifices that would be made on the altar prior to giving Eli her son. Not only was she faithful, but she also had an attitude of worship and praise in the midst of a difficult situation. Hannah's actions challenge us to be trustworthy of God's blessings. We must strive to be positive and have an attitude of worship when we give back to God, rather than becoming hostile and begrudging.

Faithfulness requires consistency. Our society is often transitory, and so is our faith experience. Hannah's faithfulness was not strong one day, and then weak the next. When we are persistent in our faithfulness, great things happen. Hannah's steadfastness produced great fruit in her son Samuel. He grew up to become a key figure in the leadership of Israel.

In Chapter 2, Hannah prayed a prayer of gratitude, known as Hannah's prayer. It cites God's goodness in her life. Her connection to Samuel did not end when she gave him to Eli the priest. In 1 Samuel 2:18, we learn that Hannah saw her son annually when she and Elkanah went to Shiloh to make sacrifice. In return, Eli, the priest, blessed the couple; and they became the parents of three additional sons and two daughters. A loving relationship with God requires faithfulness. Like Hannah, we must strive to remain faithful during the good as well as the difficult, times.

Reflecting and Recording

Can God trust you with a blessing?

Hannah worshiped God in the temple during two troubling times. What enabled her to praise the Lord despite her sorrow?

Spend time today reflecting on what life was like for Hannah. Write a few sentences that describe her acts of trusting God despite her pain. How you can do the same.

DAY SEVEN: GROUP MEETING

Prepare for the meeting by thinking back over your readings and reflections for the week and what you would like to share with the group. You might ponder such questions as these:

♦ As you imagined what it would be like to walk a mile in this woman's shoes, what lessons have you learned from studying the story of this remarkable biblical woman?

♦ How were you strengthened as well as challenged by this story?

♦ What insights have you gained about God from reading about this woman and her relationship with God? How did God act in her life? How has God acted in similar ways in your own life?

♦ What have these stories inspired you to do? How will you put what you have learned into practice?

Pray for the members of your group. Pray that you will be open and receptive to hearing what they have to say as well as what God is saying to you in your time together.

Week Six:
The Widow With the Oil—
Hanging On
Until Your Miracle Comes

Readings for the Week: 2 Kings 4:1-7

DAY ONE: REMAINING FAITHFUL
WHEN THERE IS NO MIRACLE IN SIGHT

2 Kings 4:1

*Now the wife of a member of the company of prophets cried to Elisha,
"Your servant my husband is dead; and you know that your servant feared
the LORD, but a creditor has come to take my two children as slaves."*

The air was thick with panic and fear. Debtors had come to seize the
widow's two sons because she could not pay what was owed. The pain
this widow experienced as she watched her children on the verge of being
sold as servants to debtors is difficult for us to fathom. This woman has
a testimony like no other, and her story makes us face this incomprehen-
sible drama. Welcome to the world of the widow with the oil. It is a
world where the selling of loved ones to settle debt was a common occurrence. Exodus 21:7 offers the basics for selling sons and daughters, while
Leviticus 25:39 discusses the selling of a brother into servanthood.
However common the practice, it must have been a distressing experience.

The widow's husband was a prophet who had been affiliated with the
great prophet Elisha. Perhaps her husband was even a member of Elisha's
training program. The family probably barely scraped by on the small
income that was donated from the public. According to biblical man-

dates, prophets could not earn a salary; and Old Testament women did not work outside the home. After her husband's death, the costs of supporting a family mounted, debts accumulated, and the widow found herself overwhelmed financially. She turned to her husband's mentor Elisha for help.

The widow knew that Elisha was a miracle worker, and she desperately needed a miracle. Elisha was a man of many miracles. In Chapter 4, we are told that he raised a child from the dead, neutralized poisonous food, and gave a barren couple a child. He was the correct source to seek.

This week, we will learn that the ability to abide until your miracle comes is a practice of faith. Waiting requires *strength*. Continually believing requires *hope*. *Steadfastness* prevents giving up and wandering away. The widow had all of these qualities and more. Her story shows us that there may be instances when we have few monetary resources, and yet our spiritual resources will sustain us.

Miracles are not ancient history and should not be relegated only to biblical times. Miracles continue to happen. I have experienced miracles in my own life. I *know* they were miracles because only God could have turned those situations completely around. Refusals have become approvals, negative responses have become positive affirmations, and desperate times have become joyous times. In each situation, faith was the key. As Hebrews 11:1 says, "Now faith is the assurance of things hoped for, the conviction of things not seen." With each situation or problem I encountered, I admitted that I could not help myself; then I got excited about a God who could. Each situation turned around when God stepped in and handled things. The widow too was caught in a difficult position, but she did not give up or give in. She realized that her God was able to help. God is also ready and able to help you.

Reflecting and Recording

What miracles have you seen in your life or the lives of others?

What issues threaten to undermine your faith?

What can help you hold on to hope until your miracle comes?

DAY TWO: ASKING FOR HELP

2 Kings 4:1

The widow approached the prophet Elisha with fervor. She cried out to Elisha, concisely laid out her dilemma, and begged him to help her. She said: "Your servant, my husband is dead; and you know that your servant feared the LORD, but a creditor has come to take my two children as slaves."

The widow was not embarrassed or hesitant to make her request. She had an emergency, and there was no time for formalities. As a destitute widow, she had no other sources for help. The social security system and insurance policies usually soften the cruel blow of a spouse's death today; but the widow had no one to turn to except her husband's mentor. She knew that Elisha was more than able to help her. The widow offers us an example of the importance of knowing where to go for help.

Perhaps our lives would be less stressful if we more readily asked for help when we need it. God has placed people around us to bless our journey; yet too often our pride gets in the way, and we fail to notice them. Sometimes pride will not allow us to open our mouths and ask for what we need. Proverbs 16:18 tells us that "pride goes before destruction." As a result we sometimes suffer needlessly when help may often be nearby. That almost happened to me as a new pastor. After a handful of mistakes, I realized that I needed a mentor to guide me. I was ashamed to ask, since

I did not want to seem needy or deficient. Moreover, I worried about what others would think. Later, I realized that people judge us whether we ask for help or not. To motivate myself, I visualized what could happen if I refused to ask for guidance. I saw myself continuing to make mistakes unnecessarily. To prevent this, I reached out to an older, wiser, and more experienced pastor. In response I received sound counsel and followed the advice; and my mistakes decreased.

The widow asked for help knowing that God would provide for her. Her faith played a major part in her ability to ask for help. She believed that God was with her even though circumstances seemed stacked against her. Unfortunately, for many people things work out in the opposite way. They may be so affected by their negative circumstances that they become discouraged and stubbornly refuse to ask for the help they need.

However, asking for help can lead to unexpected blessings. Jesus encourages us to bring our problems to him rather than trying to make it on our own or solve them ourselves. Trusting God is the key to doing this. Jesus told us: "Ask, and it will be given you; . . . knock, and the door will be opened for you" (Matthew 7:7).

Reflecting and Recording

List areas where you need help, then list persons who might be able to provide that help.

What role does pride play in your ability to ask for help?

Have there been situations where you have focused on what others think more than on what God thinks? How did that affect your actions and the situation? What might you have done differently?

DAY THREE: WHAT YOU HAVE IS ENOUGH FOR GOD

2 Kings 4:2

Elisha said to her, "What shall I do for you? Tell me, what do you have in the house?" She answered, "Your servant has nothing in the house, except a jar of oil."

After the widow begged Elisha to help her, he asked her a poignant and powerful question; "What do you have in the house?" In the frantic days after her husband's death, possessions such as clothing, furniture, and animals had to be sold. She thought for a minute then answered, "Your servant has nothing in the house, except a jar of oil." She had nothing but oil, which she offered only half-heartedly, believing that it wasn't very valuable. Oil was a staple in her world, and she had only a small amount of it at that. Perhaps she felt that if she owned a pair of golden earrings or fine purple linens like the wealthy women in the village, then she would have something of value. Even a goat or a bull would be a more fitting offering. Instead, all she had was a humble jar of oil.

The prophet's question was intended to force the widow to look within herself and discover what was already there. We often seek help from an outside source, without searching within to determine our own strengths and abilities. We may see only sadness and sorrow inside ourselves, and assume that the view is better elsewhere. We erroneously believe that someone else has the right answer to our problems. Although others can sometimes point us in the right direction, a look within may be what we most need to reveal God's work in our situation.

Elisha also asked the question as a means of illustrating the greatness of God. He knew that as the widow looked into her own life, she would witness God performing a miracle. Often God makes use of the smallest things in our lives and turns them into large things. God specializes in making much from little. My mother has similar skills in the kitchen. It amazes me how she can rummage through the refrigerator and cabinets, transforming remnants and leftovers of food into majestic meals. She has a knack for knowing how to combine small amounts of this and that, and present them as complete appetizing meals. My mother is not deterred by the size of the leftover. Nothing is too small; she finds a way to make it useful and tasty. God is the same way. What we have is never too small or insignificant.

The widow's discovery of God's awesome abilities is equally true for our lives. Sometimes we discount what we have to offer because we don't believe it is acceptable—whether it is our family background, level of education, the car we drive, or the house we live in. Self-imposed limitations push God out of the equation and suggest that we can achieve based only on what we have. The widow's unassuming jar of oil should liberate our thinking and remind us that God specializes in doing the impossible. Remember, Adam was formed from clay scooped from the earth (Genesis 2:7). Never doubt what God can do with the smallest items in your life.

Reflecting and Recording

Ask yourself the same question that Elisha asked the widow: What do you have in the house? Replace the words *the house* with the word *you.*

What do you have to offer to God?

Are you resisting or running from opportunities because you feel that you lack something? If so, with what do you want God's help?

DAY FOUR: IT MIGHT NOT MAKE SENSE

2 Kings 4:3

[Elisha] said, "Go outside, borrow vessels from all your neighbors, empty vessels and not just a few."

Have you ever been asked to do something that did not make sense? Has anyone ever made an outrageous request of you that defied all logic? Elisha instructed the widow to do something that simply did not make sense. After she offered her humble jar of oil, he instructed her to "borrow vessels from all [her] neighbors," then he added, "empty vessels and not just a few." This command seemed like nonsense on the surface. Besides, it was probably embarrassing to ask for empty oil jars. The neighbors would ridicule her. They might even question her sanity and wonder why God would place her in such an awkward position.

The request, however, made lots of sense to God and to those who believe in God. God often moves in directions that typical logic cannot comprehend. When God is at work in *your* life, things will likely not make sense then either. You will find yourself doing things, saying things, and going places that you never imagined. You may even experience a feeling of diminished control in your life. Relax. This is simply God taking over.

When God called me into ordained ministry, it did not make sense. It was confusing and frightening, and it seemed a ridiculous request. I was concerned about how my family and friends would react. My career path was going in an entirely different direction, and ordained ministry was *not* in my plans. God's instructions did not add up. As a believer, I had to trust and lean on God completely. Most important, I realized that I couldn't figure out God's plan for me. It was, and is, impossible, because God says, "My thoughts are not your thoughts, / nor are your ways my ways" (Isaiah 55:8).

God's plan did not make sense to the widow either, but she realized that God knew best. As she knocked on each neighbor's door and asked for empty jars, she moved closer to her miracle. Her obedience to God made the difference. Her faith was not hampered by what seemed to be a ridiculous request. If she had not been a true believer, she might have simply dismissed Elisha and his command. She may have thought he was making light of her problems. Her story demonstrates that faith makes sense of nonsense situations. We know that God would never hurt or harm us. Miracles are not explainable. If they were, they would not be miracles.

Our world prompts us to get to the bottom of everything in order to obtain a detailed explanation of what has happened. Sometimes we refuse to take another step forward in our faith journey until the way is clear and all the options have been explained. This is a mistake, because it presumes that God needs to offer us an explanation about our lives and experiences. Instead we must be brave enough to trust, and then get out of the way and let God act.

Reflecting and Recording

How have you responded to requests from God that did not make sense?

How has the widow helped you understand miracles?

Why does God ask us to do difficult things?

DAY FIVE: BEHIND CLOSED DOORS

2 Kings 4:4-6

*Then go in, and shut the door behind you and your children, and
start pouring into all these vessels; when each is full, set it aside."
So she left him and shut the door behind her and her children; they kept
bringing vessels to her, and she kept pouring. When the vessels were full,
she said to her son, "Bring me another vessel." But he said to her,
"There are no more." Then the oil stopped flowing.*

After the widow and her children had gathered the empty vessels from
their neighbors, their next step toward the miracle was to go behind
closed doors and begin pouring oil from her original jar. They poured
and poured and poured the oil into the empty jars. Although the initial
amount of oil seemed small, it yielded enough to fill many jars.
Eventually the widow's son declared all the vessels were full: "There are
no more" (verse 6). At that point the oil stopped flowing. The miracle
was that the small amount of oil became a large amount. The widow had
the faith to begin pouring, and God blessed her by providing the oil to
pour.

The miracle was cloaked in secrecy because outsiders may have dis-
counted the faith that was required. Her neighbors and even her family
might have doubted God's ability to produce a miracle. They were not
invited. It was nothing personal; but everyone is not ready to receive or

even believe in miracles, which is perhaps why God performed a private miracle. Throughout the Bible we read about two types of miracles. There were public miracles for entire groups, like the parting of the Red Sea; and private miracles for only a few, like the miraculous, multiplying oil. In this instance, God's miracle was only for the widow and her two children. Jesus also performed private miracles as well as public miracles. At times, he even instructed some of the people whom he had healed to tell no one.

Crowds and large groups can be difficult places in which to practice your faith. Lots of emotions and beliefs are present that can cause confusion. Moreover, everyone in a group is not necessarily a believer. Crowds have a tendency to influence our reactions and behavior. When we are being watched or observed, we oftentimes will alter our behavior. In private, we are generally more relaxed, at ease, and willing to be our true selves. God wants time with our true selves.

The lesson here is that we should never hesitate to spend time alone with the Lord. Community worship is an important part of our spiritual development, but the time we spend alone with God is particularly special. We benefit greatly from one-on-one time with God. On these occasions, God can talk to us and us alone. God desires alone time with us to establish a sweet communion. Unfortunately, our lives and our time are so limited or overrun by scheduled tasks and activities that God is either placed last on the list or omitted altogether. Instead, God desires personal, private time with us: "Whenever you pray, go into your room and shut the door and pray to your Father who is in secret; and your Father who sees in secret will reward you" (Matthew 6:6).

Reflecting and Recording

Could you have had the faith to pour from the widow's original jar of oil knowing there was not much in it?

How does a crowd affect your worship experience?

How much time alone do you spend with God? How does this time enhance and enrich your spiritual life?

DAY SIX: LIVE ON THE REST

2 Kings 4:7

She came and told the man of God, and he said, "Go sell the oil and pay your debts, and you and your children can live on the rest."

The widow ran back to the prophet. This time she cried out with joy as she related her miracle to him. The many borrowed vessels of oil were full! He told her, "Go sell the oil and pay your debts" (verse 7). What a joyous time this was! All of the financial misery that surrounded her was gone. The threat of losing her children was over; and most important, she had an encounter with God that blessed her mightily. She may have laughed, danced, and cried tears of joy all at once. Those neighbors who gave her empty vessels may have come outside to see what was going on. Perhaps they joined in her joy, because now they too could understand the power of God.

The prophet commanded her to take another step in faith when he said, "You and your children can live on the rest" (verse 7). In fact, he was urging her to allow God's blessing to meet both her financial and spiritual needs. Of course, the money she earned selling the oil handled the living expenses for her family; but God desired to do more than simply meet financial needs. God wanted to care for *all* of her needs. To "live on the rest" also meant that God wanted her to have peace and joy for the remainder of her life. The prophet was pronouncing a blessing on her life that she would be covered and cared for by God forever.

God is looking for a permanent relationship with us beyond the time of our miracle as well. For some, a miracle is too often the first time they truly believe that God cares about them. Once God gets our attention through a miracle, God wants to move deeper into our lives. Our spiritual needs are particularly important. God is our provider and our sustainer. God is always about the business of taking care of us. Our every need and concern matter to God. Perhaps during the time of the Old Testament, women more readily allowed God to sustain them because societal customs dictated that they could not support themselves. As modern women, we have access to numerous forms of support; so we may find relying on God to meet our needs challenging. However, the quality of life that we have depends on what sustains us or keeps us going. God is the only unchanging force in our world.

It is interesting to note that the widow did not meet God face to face in her miracle. Instead God met her in the oil that flowed so abundantly. This shows that God can meet us in any circumstance, situation, or person of God's choosing. We must be open and receptive to God's blessings in unusual places. We might meet God while buying groceries or even at the hair salon. God is with us everywhere, ever ready to become part of who we are.

The abundance of the widow's blessing is also encouragement for us to trust God for blessings that are so large we do not have room for them. Our God is generous beyond measure and equally as creative. Get ready for your miracle. God wants to bless you. Be prepared. Your miracle may amaze you. Remember these words from 1 Corinthians 2: 9: " 'What no eye has seen, nor ear heard / nor the human heart conceived, / what God has prepared for those who love him'— / these things God has revealed to us through the Spirit."

Reflecting and Recording

God wants to take care of you. Will you allow God to do that? How?

Are you ready for your miracle? How do you know that you are ready?

Spend time today reading and praying about the life of the widow with the oil. Write a few sentences that describe her ability to wait until her miracle came. How can you do the same?

DAY SEVEN: GROUP MEETING

Prepare for the meeting by thinking back over your readings and reflections for the week and what you would like to share with the group. You might ponder such questions as these:

♦ As you imagined what it would be like to walk a mile in this woman's shoes, what lessons have you learned from studying the story of this remarkable biblical woman?

♦ How were you strengthened as well as challenged by this story?

♦ What insights have you gained about God from reading about this woman and her relationship with God? How did God act in her life? How has God acted in similar ways in your own life?

♦ What have these stories inspired you to do? How will you put what you have learned into practice?

Pray for the members of your group. Pray that you will be open and receptive to hearing what they have to say as well as what God is saying to you in your time together.